MW01617183

SEEDS OF GENEROSITY

Seeds

of
Generosity

Storytelling in the Classroom

Stories selected and introduced by

MARGO MCLOUGHLIN

Published by Salsbury House Press, Victoria, BC,
in partnership with the Fetzer Institute

© Copyright Margo McLoughlin, 2012. All rights reserved.
Published by Salsbury House Press, Victoria, BC, in partnership with the Fetzer Institute

Margo McLoughlin
Victoria, BC
margostoryteller@gmail.com

Library and Archives Canada Cataloguing in Publication

Seeds of generosity : storytelling in the classroom / edited by Margo McLouglin.
Includes bibliographical references.

ISBN 978-0-9916880-0-5

1. Storytelling in education. 2. Generosity. 3. Tales. I. McLoughlin, Margo, 1960–.

LB1042M35 2012   372.67´7042   C2012-9059498-8

Permissions acknowledgements may be found on pages 102-103.

We gratefully acknowledge the support of the Fetzer Institute in the creation and publication of this book.

Illustrations by Jennah Vhay Fox
Cover illustration by Judy Levine (judymlevine.com)
Edited by Leslie Kenny
Proofread by Carol Neufeld
Design and layout by Vancouver Desktop Publishing Centre Ltd.
Printed on 100% recycled paper in Canada by Printorium Bookworks

*To my parents, with much love
and to Maguy, for the gift of stories*

Contents

Preface

When I think of my early school years I remember very little of what happened within the walls of the classroom, except for one thing—listening to the stories my teacher told. I didn't know, of course, that her storytelling would prove to have such a significant impact in my life. In 1968, the small independent school I attended in Vancouver launched one of the first experiments in bilingual education in the country. Housed in a separate building—a stately old home on the corner of the school property—the Bilingual-Bicultural Program had hired teachers from France and Quebec. My teacher was an elegant young Parisienne named Maguy Duchesne. A born storyteller who showed little concern for the conventions of prescribed curriculum, Maguy enthralled us with stories of growing up in France during the Second World War. These were long, involved narratives, every word of which we took to be the truth. There were twists and turns and unexpected reversals, but the guiding themes were the pursuit of justice and the challenge of knowing the right thing to do.

Life was a great adventure. This is what Maguy imparted through her stories. From listening to Maguy and reading all the adventure books I could find, I began to ask myself, What am I going to do? What will be my role in benefiting the world? My vocational aspirations included spy, translator, and writer of children's adventure stories. (Note: I have never been employed as a spy, but I did settle in Quebec during the height of the separatist movement with the express intention of convincing Quebecers to vote against separation. This plan backfired, however, when I learned the history of oppression in Quebec. I ended up voting *oui* in the referendum.) Making my way into adult life, I may have forgotten the content of the stories I heard, but I never forgot the meaning of the storytelling experience. I do believe it was those stories that nourished my sense of adventure and oriented me towards compassionate action.

I grew up and became a teacher myself. I volunteered in Africa. In my 20s, I rediscovered storytelling. At a silent retreat with the Buddhist teacher Thich Nhat Hanh a friend called my attention to another retreat participant, a woman with snowy white hair and a youthful face. "That's Mary Love May," she said. "She's a storyteller." "A storyteller!" I said. "What's that?" Later I realized I knew perfectly well what a storyteller was. But at the time, it struck me as a strange and wonderful occupation. The day after the retreat ended I happened to be looking out the window of my apartment when I saw Mary Love May entering the elementary school across the street. I called the school, told them I was a neighbour, and asked if I could attend the storytelling that was about to take place in their library. I was invited to come along, and so I did. I helped Mary Love May set up the chairs in a half-circle and watched as she drew the children into the magical realm of Story. Reflecting on the experience later, I felt that I had witnessed something very beautiful, very ancient, and very simple, as if the skill of drawing water from a well had been lost and then found again. As I observed the stillness and attention of the listening children in that school library, I knew that storytelling was all about generosity.

I have now been telling stories for more than twenty years. When I began to call myself a storyteller, friends would ask me when I was holding my next "reading." "There will be no reading involved," I would say. "Because I won't be reading the story, I'll be telling it!" It was an important distinction to me. Whether I was telling stories in the classroom as a teacher, or whether I was performing at a festival in the role of storyteller, I had seen how the oral nature of storytelling helped me create an immediate relationship with my listeners. In the co-creation of the story experience special bonds of connection were being formed. I know that other storytellers and storytelling teachers have had the experience of returning to a classroom or school where children have received the gift of their stories. It is remarkable how children remember those stories and will run up to say hello. It reminds me to honour my gift and keep on telling stories!

In 2003, while completing my studies for a Master of Divinity at the Harvard Divinity School, I was one of several researchers hired by the Fetzer Institute's Generosity of Spirit project. The initial aim of the project was to explore how the world's many cultures use stories to teach this quality of heart and mind we call generosity of spirit. I put together a database of over two hundred folktales. With my colleague Ian Simmons, I compiled an anthology, still unpublished, titled "The Secret of Dreaming: Tales of Generosity from Around the World" with 75 of the stories, arranged by stage of life. Subsequently, the Generosity of Spirit project began using the stories in community settings.[1]

Meanwhile, I began looking for opportunities to use the stories with children. I tried them out in an English as a Second Language program in Watertown, Massachusetts and later in an after-school program in East Boston. Over the past year (2011–2012), while I was at the Centre for Studies in Religion and Society at the University of Victoria, I designed an eight-week school series using the generosity stories. Once a week I visited two Grade Four classrooms to tell a story

---

1   More about the Generosity of Spirit pilot retreats can be found in *The Giving Heart: Folktales for Exploring Generosity*, by Margo McLoughlin (Victoria, BC: Salsbury House Press, 2012).

and lead a short discussion with the children. In one class, the children kept a story journal, in which they reflected on the stories, suggested titles, or summarized the events. Some months after my last visit, I returned and gave the children an oral quiz to see what they remembered about the stories. It was surprising how clearly they recalled phrases, characters, and the principal meaning they had taken from the tale. My goal was to see if the children found the stories and the storytelling experience enjoyable and relevant. From my review of their journals and from my conversation with the children I would say the answer is yes, they did. However, the fact that I was a visitor who only appeared once a week for less than an hour did limit the impact of the storytelling experience. Because I wasn't with the children every day I had no way of knowing how the story might relate to their daily lives. I wasn't there to refer to it, or to encourage them to retell it themselves. I realized that the best person for children to hear stories from is the one they see every day—their teacher or their parent. Why? Because then the story becomes part of a shared language. The story's potential as a metaphor depends on all the members of the group knowing it. Also, the principal gift of storytelling is that it makes space for relationships to develop. In the shared experience of the story, children become a tribe of listeners, dependent on each other to protect the storytelling space from intrusions and distractions. There is no doubt that storytelling builds community. It creates a time of respect and attention. What we discover is that for the storytelling to work, each member of the group needs to be fully present. It is both the generosity of the teller and the generosity of the listeners that allow the story's images to be like seeds borne on the wind to fertile soil.

The aim of this book is to invite teachers and parents to build relationships through storytelling, while exploring this beautiful quality which is generosity.

Margo McLoughlin
Victoria, BC
August, 2012

PART I

EDUCATING THE HEART

ONE

GENEROSITY AND STORYTELLING

I t is the aim of this book to encourage classroom teachers, educators of all stripes, and parents to *tell stories*, drawing on their life experience for material, or choosing folktales to tell, but aiming to turn the television off, put the book down, and let the story take wing between one heart and another, and between minds and hearts. At the same time, we can encourage a storytelling culture in the classroom and at home by inviting children to share their own stories and creating the space to receive them.

Educating the Heart

What does it mean to educate the heart? It means creating new kinds of learning experiences within the structure of the school setting. It means strengthening and developing children's natural ability to see patterns and connections in human relationships. It means encouraging children to see themselves as capable of making a difference.

We live in an interconnected world. Educating the heart is about opening to this truth. By allowing the wisdom of the heart to guide our actions we discover that we *can* make a difference, both to our own happiness and to the happiness of others. We can join hearts and hands to support the healing of our beleaguered planet. Nourishing children's imagination with storytelling and stories is an important part of this journey.

Generosity and Storytelling

Stories about giving and receiving remind us that generosity is both a practice and a path of discovery. It is a practice that can be nurtured every day. Like any practice, the more it is nurtured and encouraged, the more it grows. It is a path of discovery because of the many insights that come to us through giving and receiving. Think of a young child in your life who has presented you with a gift—a half-eaten cookie, a wet leaf, an artful scribble. The child's delight in offering something with her own hands increases the moment we light up and receive the gift. This may give rise to the child's first insight into generosity—the recognition that we are capable of affecting another person in small but significant ways. Happiness is ours to give.

And, as we know from our own experience with children, developing a generous heart is also about receiving what is offered. Intuitively, we know that open-hearted receiving is what keeps the energy of the gift in circulation.[2] A gift, in many cultures, is only temporarily ours. The notion of ownership is absent and therefore no gift is burdensome to receive. The object that is given remains in the possession of the receiver for a shorter or longer time, until it is needed by someone else. Folktales present this in stark terms. Those who refuse the gift or disparage it find their fortunes blocked, just as the cycle of giving has been blocked. Those who receive the gift, whatever it is, see their fortunes transformed. In the first folktale in this collection, an Indian tale called "A Drum," a young boy receives a series of gifts, none of which is what he wants, yet his openness to receiving what is offered ultimately leads him to the cherished drum he asked for.

Another discovery that happens along the path of giving is a growing awareness of the power we have to make significant choices, to reach beyond the range of our usual concerns and include others in our thoughts and hearts. Discovering this potential can unleash enormous energy and creativity. Many examples come to mind, but one that stands out is the story of Ryan Hreljac, a six-year-old boy in Ontario who raised money to provide a well for villagers in Uganda. Ryan's vision and commitment inspired the members of his community to uncover their own generosity and help him meet his goal.[3]

Developing our capacity to give is an investment in our present and future happiness. Gradually, it becomes a habit that informs every aspect of our lives. To be patient is to be generous. To listen with one's full attention is an extraordinary gift. To share ideas and collaborate is to practice generosity. To forgive oneself and others is true generosity of spirit. And when we consider stewardship of the planet as our priority, we are offering a gift to future generations. Stories about giving and receiving and the storytelling experience itself offer many ways to educate the heart by exploring what it means to live a generous life.

The Case for Story

We often think of stories as having moral lessons that will serve us on our path through life. However, if learning the lesson in the story becomes our focus, we may have missed the real gift in storytelling. Beyond morals and lessons, the real learning received by the listeners is that someone has time for them—time to enrich their imagination with images, ideas and questions from their own, time to tune in to their experience of a story. We don't realize how critical this form of

---

2   See Lewis Hyde, *The Gift: Creativity and the Artist in the Modern World.* (New York: Vintage Books, 1979 and 2007).

3   Since its formation in 2001, Ryan's Well Foundation has helped build 713 water projects and 911 latrines, bringing safe water and improved sanitation to 750,991 people. See www.ryanswell.ca.

engagement is in children's development. Oral storytelling creates the space for the mutual listening and emotional tracking that allows us to become "friends of one another's minds."[4]

Even as our leading neuroscientists and educators are advocating new ways of thinking about education that are based on face-to-face relationship building, our culture is turning out more ways to isolate people from one another. We have an extreme fascination with novelty and choice, especially in the realm of technology. Interactive whiteboards are appearing in classrooms, allowing teachers to show videos and access photos, maps, and images from the Internet. Soon, it appears, teachers will be moving to the sidelines, where they can direct the "screen" experience.

However, there isn't yet an invention that will take the place of Story. Of course, you can listen to recorded versions of stories, a wonderful form of entertainment. But that's not what I mean by Story. Story is the experience and gift of presence. It is hearing a person's voice in real time. It is feeling that person's presence and involvement in both the narrative and the narration. The storyteller may be telling a folktale, a made-up story, a family story, or a memory from her own life. What marks the difference between a recorded version and a live version is the dynamic connection between teller and listener, expressed through a form of listening that goes both ways. When I am telling a story to my students I am constantly attending to their level of interest and engagement. I want to make sure that all of them can "see" the story in their imagination, so I am listening with my whole being, even as I'm telling. What does their body language tell me about their involvement? What do their faces tell me? I may even stop the story to say, "What do you think will happen next?" A parent reading from a book will do the same thing, adjusting her tone of voice or pacing as she senses her listener's mood. The story experience is a collaboration.

"The experiences we have actually shape the brain," says child psychiatrist and educator Dr. Daniel Siegel in his book *MindSight*.[5] He describes two sets of circuits in the brain, one of which allows us to interact with the physical world and another that engages the mind, developing our capacity to reflect, to be in relationship, and to stay present with whatever is happening. Traditional curricula and teaching have been focused on the circuits that are necessary for physical survival. Dr. Siegel describes the need for a "circuitry of kindness," "neurons of compassion," and ways to realize we are part of a functional whole.[6] We don't need to throw out the three

---

4   Maxine Greene. Foreword, in Carol Witherell and Nel Noddings, eds., *Stories Lives Tell: Narrative and Dialogue in Education* (New York: Teachers College Press, 1991).

5   Dr. Siegel is a child psychiatrist, educator, and executive director of the MindSight Institute.

6   "The Power of MindSight," from a TedXBlue Talk recorded October 18, 2009. http://www.youtube.com/watch?v=Nu7wEr8AnHw

Rs, he says, referring to Reading, 'Riting, and 'Rithmetic; we just need to add three more Rs—Reflection, Relationships, and Resilience.

Dr. Siegel has coined the term "mindsight" to describe the process of becoming aware of our own mental and emotional experience as well as that of others. He writes:

> How we focus our attention shapes the structure of the brain. Neuroscience supports the idea that developing the reflective skills of mindsight activates the very circuits that create resilience and well-being and that underlie empathy and compassion as well.[7]

Dr. Siegel explains how the neural circuits that underlie the skill of mindsight need experiences to develop properly.

> . . . [T]he ability to see the mind develops through everyday interactions with others, especially through attentive communication with parents and caregivers. When adults are in tune with a child, when they reflect back to the child an accurate picture of his internal world, he comes to sense his own mind with clarity. This is the foundation of mindsight.[8]

Storytelling offers just such an experience of attentive communication. It is a gift of loving attention as well as a model of how to give this same gift. To become generous, empathetic beings, we need models of generosity and empathy. We need to have been nourished by loving relationships and to have seen our own potential reflected in another. Stories and storytelling are at the heart of this form of attentive communication because stories provide a framework for making sense of human experience, for recognizing the different perspectives on experience that are possible, and for sparking the imagination with the capacity to dream.

Storytelling and Resilience

This brings me to the case for repetition. A good story is worth retelling, rereading, and re-entering many times. A good story is worth knowing so well that it becomes an old friend. And, taken one step further, a story that is repeatedly entered and fully imagined becomes part of our own story. It shapes how we see the world. When a child hears the same story more than once, she is also learning something very important about the flexible human mind. For even when a story is read aloud from a book and especially when it is told orally, the story is never exactly the same. Unlike the dialogue and images in a video, the unique beauty of the storytelling depends on many conditions, including the make-up of the audience, the weather, the energy of the teller, and the actual physical surroundings. Each one

---

7   Daniel J. Siegel, *Mindsight: The New Science of Personal Transformation* (New York: Bantam Books, 2011), p. xiii.

8   Siegel, *Mindsight*, p. xv.

of these factors, and many others, will make a difference to the way the story is told. Through the direct experience of many tellings, a child learns that telling stories is about relating to the present moment in a dynamic way. This is what's happening now, and this is how the story goes . . .

Storytelling builds resilience. Nourished by a core group of stories, children develop the ability to imagine their own lives. Dr. Robert Coles writes about a young woman named Delia who had a child of her own at fourteen and who felt trapped in the violent subculture of her community. In his conversations with Delia, Coles learned about her grandmother, who only had one book, the Bible, and who loved to tell her grandchildren Bible stories. Delia's imagination was nourished both by the stories her grandmother told her and by her presence. But when Delia was nine years old, her grandmother was killed in the crossfire of a gang shootout. In describing Delia, Coles writes that she had a "moral imagination that had never been nourished, at least since her grandmother died." As Coles points out, Delia needed to hear her grandmother's stories and feel that connection many more times in order to make those stories her own. Then, as a young adult, she would have been better able to fully imagine her own future.[9]

Storytelling in the Classroom

The challenge in any group is to build relationships based on shared experience and shared values. Storytelling can offer that shared experience. World tales of giving and receiving offer a rich variety of entry points to explore the value of generosity. Little by little, and story by story, a hodge-podge of boys and girls from different backgrounds and with different interests, become a community of tellers and listeners. Vivian Paley writes:

> In a cohesive society, family, or classroom, each member is storyteller and story listener by turn as the train of events moves along a shared network of daily expectations and surprises, histories and fantasies, laws and customs.[10]

In *Seeds of Generosity: Storytelling in the Classroom* you will find a selection of stories from the world's wisdom traditions. Choose a handful to tell over the course of the school year, one a month or even one every two months. If you retell them enough, work with them, illustrate scenes from them, and reflect on them in discussions, they will become part of the children's framework for viewing the world and their

---

9 Robert Coles, *The Moral Intelligence of Children* (New York: Random House, 1997).

10 Vivian Paley, "Looking for Magpie: Another Voice in the Classroom," in *Narrative in Teaching, Learning, and Research*, Hunter McEwan and Kieran Egan, eds. (New York:Teachers College Press, 1995), p. 95.

place in it. What better gift could we give children than a rich assortment of stories to think with and grow with?

Each group of folktales in this book addresses a particular theme, and includes a handful of questions for follow-up discussions. Before we dive into the stories, however, the next section explores four different modes of storytelling.

TWO

FOUR WAYS TO THINK ABOUT STORYTELLING

The truth about stories is that that's all we are.

—THOMAS KING

Story is the essential culture builder and learning tool of any society or family or classroom. The child within us and the children in our classes yearn for stories. It matters not that we no longer sit around campfires originating mythology—or even spend much time on porches gossiping and spinning tales—every child re-enacts this ancient means of expression and depends on its form to explain life's deepest concerns.

—VIVIAN PALEY

We are made of stories *and* we are storytellers. The trouble is that we've forgotten. For the last hundred years, new modes of storytelling have replaced the oral tradition in Western cultures, casting a spell on story-lovers everywhere. From the silent movies of Buster Keaton and Charlie Chaplin, to the epic films of the Thirties and Forties to the arrival of the television in our living rooms and now to the hand-held device entrancing us with its unlimited array of search functions and helpful tools, we have fallen into the habit of relying on someone else to create our story experience for us. Luckily, it's not too late to reclaim our storytellling-nature.

Together, in classrooms and at home, we can rediscover the stories we are made of. We can grow into the storytellers we are meant to be, telling jokes and riddles, stories of mishaps and adventures, life lessons and wonder tales from our family history and our own memories.

Three Kinds of Storytelling, Plus One . . .

Oral storytelling is a unique mode of communication, but it doesn't always look the same. In fact, once we become aware of the use of narrative in our speech, it's apparent that we are frequently telling a certain kind of story—short anecdotes and accounts of our daily lives. While listening to a friend of mine speak with her three-year old daughter, I noticed that they were building a family collection of narratives by actively remembering together incidents from the recent past as well as the more distant past. They were turning life experience into stories. The second and more traditional mode of oral storytelling is the creation of a sustained experience of listening. Through the evocative use of language, voice, and presence, the teller engages the listeners in the action and emotion of the tale. The members of the audience are taken away on the wings of the narrative, temporarily losing any self-awareness or consciousness of their surroundings. A third kind of storytelling is the references we make to myth and folklore, using stories as a shorthand metaphor. "He really has the Midas touch," we say. Or, "Don't be like the boy who cried wolf."

In her study of a classroom where the teacher incorporates storytelling into her teaching, Johanna Kuyyenhoven writes about these three modes of storytelling: talking with stories, thinking with stories, and "imagining," a term coined by one of the students.[11] Each of these modes involves a unique kind of interaction between the story, the storyteller, and the story-listeners. Each interaction involves a type of giving and receiving.

Talking with Stories

Talking with stories refers to the storytelling that happens in children's conversations or in class meetings. It is informal and mostly unrehearsed. These stories are often simple anecdotes or glimpses into each other's lives. They might relate to a special object brought from home—a family treasure or photograph, or a book; or, the story may be a retelling of some current event read about in the newspaper or heard on the radio. Talking with stories is happening whenever there is telling and listening. By making space for this kind of storytelling, many important skills are being developed, including the skill of listening and sustaining one's own attention. The skill of empathy is also being developed. When children hear each other's stories on a regular basis they gain a more complete understanding of the unique circumstances of each other's lives.

On Monday morning, when children come into the classroom, they are often filled with news of their home life—the arrival of a new pet in the household, the visit of a grandparent, an older sibling's success on a sports team. Unless there is a structured time for sharing news, the enthusiasm to "tell stories" must be saved for whispered conversations, or recess. Putting off or blocking this energy to communicate

---

11   Johanna Kuyyenhoven, *In the Presence of Each Other: A Pedagogy of Storytelling* (Toronto: University of Toronto Press, 2009), pp. 52–58.

in story-form is a missed learning opportunity—for acquiring oral language skills, for developing a personal narrative style, and for learning how to listen to others.

Telling personal stories is part of developing a classroom culture. What follows are three ideas for "talking with stories" that are simple enough to incorporate into the day's routines:

News Groups

Children gather in groups of four to share their news on Monday mornings.[12] Each child has three or four minutes to describe something that happened over the weekend or holiday. The others listen and then ask questions to help the teller add detail. A bell rings to signal the turn of the next child. When all four have had a turn, the children return to their desks or to the carpet and the teacher calls on one or two to retell their story (or the story of another member of their group) for the whole class. With a bit of practice in listening and asking good questions, this exercise will give every child the opportunity to tell a story about her own life at least once a week. Gradually, even the shyest child gains confidence from the experience of sharing something about herself with classmates.

Class Meetings

In a class meeting, different children are assigned the task of bringing specific kinds of news items or stories, including sports news, current events, riddles, and jokes. Class meetings might take place once a week, once every two weeks, or more often.

At the End of the Day

Together children can recall something about the day: a visitor, a change in the weather, a fire drill, an object lost then found, the completion of a group project, a school ceremony. Taking turns, the children provide their own descriptions, adding sensory details. (Example: "I had to stand on the bench during the choir rehearsal and I felt hot and squished.") This form of group storytelling could lead to journal writing or to the creation of a class newsletter or magazine. A storytelling friend of mine who is an experienced teacher of Waldorf education, described a similar activity in her classroom where children shared an image from their day: a crow landing on the playground to seize a crust of bread, the feeling of the sun on one's face, the sound of the wind in the trees.

Informal storytelling happens each time we share a scene from the narrative of our lives. By tuning into this story-making aspect of daily conversation, we see how this kind of listening and telling weaves threads of connection. We notice how one person's story triggers another's memory and launches him into his story.

---

12 I'm thinking of this exercise for children aged eight and older, but it might work with younger children as well.

Who hasn't been part of a sharing of stories about pets and their antics, disastrous holidays, eccentric relatives, or magical places?

Storytelling can seem like a poor use of classroom time when there is a lot of curriculum to be covered but it's actually quite important. Something more than idle chit-chat is happening when this kind of communication is encouraged. There is a field of generosity that is present or absent in any physical space where people interact. Intuitively we know whether our thoughts and ideas will be welcomed and whether it is safe to share who we are. Making space in the day for talking with stories allows children to be co-creators of that space. It reminds them that they have something worthwhile to share—themselves.

Entering the Story World: Imagination and Ethics

A second kind of storytelling participation is the traditional experience of hearing a story. Imagine a quiet space with one teller and many listeners. When the signal is given, the children gather quietly on the floor or the carpet. The teacher-storyteller makes sure that she can see each child from where she is sitting or standing.[13] She may use a musical instrument to evoke the story-space. She may recite a poem or a proverb. In these ways she marks off the story-time from the rest of the day. The children know they can relax. And indeed, as they drop into the story they suspend their habitual boundaries. Entering the story is akin to stepping through a gateway into another realm. As soon as they are "in" they begin to relax.[14] In a sense, what they are relaxing is the effort to be somebody in particular. Instead, they can be anybody and everybody in the unfolding sequence of events. This trance-like state is deeply engaging and deeply nourishing. In the direct encounter with the action of the story children have a place to be wise, kind, and brave, but also greedy, slow, mean, jealous, and fearful. They see, from within the story, what happens when a character is led by various motivations. The storytelling session becomes a starting place for thinking about ethics and for developing an awareness of ourselves as actors and agents in the world.

Through telling and listening to stories, we explore other perspectives. As one literary theorist writes, it is through storytelling that "we learn to make subtle and not so subtle shifts in point of view, and these shifts are crucial to developing the sense of self and others so necessary to moral agency."[15] Stories take us out of ourselves and our limited point of view. They offer us a glimpse of the world

---

13 This is important for ensuring the children's complete attention to the story and also for the teller to keep track of her listeners and their engagement.

14 Johanna Kuyyenhoven takes note of children's posture as they engage in "imagining" during a storytelling session.

15 Lynne Tirrell, "Storytelling and Moral Agency," in *Journal of Aesthetics and Art Criticism* 48: 119.

from the perspective of other beings. This experience is fundamental to awakening sympathy. By imagining what another feels, hopes, and longs for, we begin to act with the knowledge that we are both different and the same as others.

If storytelling is where the moral imagination begins to develop, it is crucial to protect the story experience and let it be just that—a gift of time shared in the parallel realm of story. There is no need for analysis or deep reflection, just appreciation. Appreciation may lead to conversation, drawing, or writing, but it doesn't have to.

Thinking With Stories: The Flexible Metaphor

Thinking with stories is the use of narrative to illustrate an abstract concept like the value of kindness or respect. The story becomes a metaphor to gain a deeper understanding of how that idea plays out in real life. Teachers may also use stories to teach about math or science, or about school policies around caring for the environment or bullying. For example, a teacher may tell a story of her own painful experience as a new student, describing how she was treated and what it felt like to be left out of games and conversations. Without laying down a hard and fast rule, the teacher has encouraged children to think about the impact of their own behavior on others.

Thinking with stories can happen in discussions that follow a storytelling experience. While the teacher may have her own view of how the elements of the folktale work as metaphors, her listeners will seize hold of the story for their own purposes. In one study, children heard a Swahili story about the trickster Hare.[16] In the folktale, Hare owns a cow. One day, he receives permission from the Sultan to leave his cow with the Sultan's bull for breeding. When a calf is born, the Sultan claims ownership of it, saying that the calf came from the bull. Hare shows how ridiculous it is to think that male animals can give birth. The Sultan is forced to let Hare take both the cow and the calf.

The author of the study, Donna Eder, asked the children, "Who would you be in the story?" Two of the children chose the calf, which is only mentioned briefly and has no agency. However, by placing themselves in the story, the children assigned agency to the calf and said that *they* would decide which parent they wanted to stay with, the cow or the bull. By asking, "Who would you be?" Donna gave the children a way of imagining other outcomes to their own life circumstances, one in which children have the right to choose which parent they will live with after a divorce.

Folktales offer children real tools to think about their own lives, especially when there is space for discussion and reflection in a small group. Asking open-

---

16 Donna Eder, with Regina Holyan, *Life Lessons through Storytelling: Children's Exploration of Ethics* (Bloomington, Indiana University Press, 2010), p. 16.

ended questions invites thinking that allows for many possibilities. As they listen to each other respond to the story, children experience a wide range of alternative perspectives. Thinking with stories allows for the development of acceptance and curiosity about how other people view the world.

Living the Story: Caring for Each Other, Caring for the Planet

To these three modes of storytelling I would add a fourth—living the story. Living the story is based on creating a life experience that will make for good stories. Acting on behalf of the planet is my focus here, but living the story is really about generosity in all the forms it takes. Here are a few ideas: Any simple project that requires the children to work together and make decisions can lead to the creation of individual and group stories. Ask the children questions to draw out their experiences of the activity. Invite a volunteer from a local environmental group to come and speak about his work. Ask the children to prepare questions to help the person tell his story. Afterwards, have the children tell a story together about the visit. Read stories of pioneer children's lives and compare them with school life in the twenty-first century. Consider the ways they related to the environment. In what ways were they more careful and better stewards? In which ways are we better stewards now? Brainstorm ways of contributing to the planet (reducing or eliminating garbage in the classroom; walking to school instead of driving, turning off the lights and using less electricity; being careful with school materials.) Create a class story about the changes that were made.

Oral storytelling develops listening skills. It nurtures empathy, imagination, flexible thinking and creativity. By incorporating these modes of storytelling into the classroom, teachers are honouring children's life experience as well as their love of stories. At the same time, they are teaching the value of relationship. When we tell a story we give something of ourselves. When we listen, we offer the gift of our listening presence. Out of this giving and receiving of attention comes something quite remarkable—mutual appreciation and trust.

THREE

GETTING READY TO TELL

Discovering Stories of Generosity

Teachers/Parents: Explore your own history of giving and receiving. Are there stories from your life that illustrate the pleasures and pitfalls of giving? Are there stories about learning how to receive with a generous heart?

Questions to Spark Your Memories:

1) Was there a special gift you received as a child? What was it? What associations do you have with that gift? What happened to it?

2) Did you ever make or prepare a special gift for a parent or grandparent? What was it? How did you make it? How was it received?

3) Were you ever given a gift that was so strange or unusual that you didn't know what to do with it? Who gave it to you? On what occasion? What did you do with it?

4) What kinds of non-material gifts have you both received and given in your life?

5) What stories have been handed down in your family?

Steps to Creating a Good Story for Oral Storytelling:

1) Invite a friend to explore these questions with you.

2) Give yourselves time to listen to each other's stories. (Five minutes each is a good amount of time to start with.)

3) Give appreciations about what you liked in the other's story.

4) Ask questions to clarify the setting or the sequence of events.

5) Then have each person tell their story a second time.

Telling Folktales

Learning a story

Storytelling is about discovering what is meaningful to you in a story and finding out how to convey that to your listener. We are not required to memorize a text and then recite it word for word. If the source is a traditional folktale, we can be sure that many versions of the story exist, each with a slightly different choice of emphasis and language. Just as other tellers have done, we can retell the folktale in our own words (though there may be certain phrases or expressions we would want to keep.) To learn a story for telling, read it through several times or, if the story is recorded, listen to it more than once. Next put the text or recording away. Practice telling it to a willing listener. It helps to picture the story as a sequence of images, just as if you were remembering an event that happened to you.[17]

The Gift of Story

Storytelling is a gift. When we create a protected time in the busy day of the classroom to shut the door, put our pencils down, and gather on the floor for a story, we are inviting children into a world of imagination and wonder. This is valuable and important in and of itself. We have to be careful as educators not to turn every storytelling event into a lesson. A great deal of learning takes place during a storytelling session. Beyond developing listening skills and new vocabulary, children are learning that an adult in their life cares enough about them to give them this precious gift.

Following the Storytelling

Storytelling often induces a kind of dreaminess in children. The whole-hearted attention they have brought to the story-listening generates a restful state. It's important not to rush onto the next thing. Instead, storytelling sessions can be easily followed by activities that strengthen children's skills in many areas of the curriculum while building on the experience of the story.

Art

The children have just been imagining the story in their own minds. Drawing a scene from the story is a natural way for them to continue working with the questions and issues the story raised. Have paper and art supplies ready, so that they can move quietly to the next activity.

---

17   These ideas come from storytelling coach Doug Lipman. See *Improving Your Storytelling: Beyond the Basics for All Who Tell Stories in Work or Play* (Little Rock, Arkansas: August House, 1999).

Writing

For older children, give them an opportunity to reflect on the story in writing. Simple questions can help get them started:

- *What title would you give to this story? Why?*

- *Who would you be in this tale?*

- *What do you think happened next?*

- *What do you think happened before the story began?*

- *What questions do you have about this story? Choose one and explore your own answer.*

Drama

The children can act out scenes from the story, creating their own dialogue. Or, they can make simple puppets and prepare props and backdrops for a puppet show.

Discussion

After the children have had several opportunities to engage with the story, gather them on the carpet or floor and retell it together. Invite reflection using any questions that the children have come up with, your own questions or the ones suggested at the end of the story.

Ideally, if the story was told at the beginning of the month or unit, it then becomes the source of several different activities over the following weeks.

WORLD TALES OF GENEROSITY

FOUR

GIVING AND RECEIVING

It will bring you a more enduring satisfaction to
give a robe to another than to wear it yourself.

—ALI IBN ABI TALIB

"Give, and it will be given to you. A good measure,
pressed down, shaken together and running over,
will be poured into your lap. For with the measure
you use, it will be measured to you.

—LUKE 6:37-38

Generosity comes from the same root as *generate* and *genus*—to give birth, to bring into existence. To practice generosity is to give birth to possibility. The creation stories of the world reflect this in the twin energies present at the moment of creation—imagination and generosity. Out of chaos or nothingness there is a spark, a welling-up of potential that seeks release in the gift of life. The mystery and complexity of existence comes into being, as life forms shape and support each other.

This is the dance of interconnectedness. In the Huayan school of Buddhism, the metaphor is a net, known as Indra's net, which hangs over Mount Meru like a great, glistening spider's web where the jewel-like dewdrops caught on each vertex reflect every other site of connection. We are mirrors for each other. We are each other's root system and source of nourishment. Giving and receiving are two facets of the same thing—the place of intersection. From the moment of our conception to our last dying breath we are inextricably linked to all of life as benefactors and as beneficiaries. Remembering this truth reminds us that our choices and our actions make a difference.

The stories in this first group of world folktales invite us to consider generosity and interconnectedness from a number of different perspectives. In "A Drum" a young boy asks for a drum and is given a stick. He willingly receives the gift and sets out to play. The gift that he bestows in each of his encounters is his interest and compassion. Seeking nothing for himself, he offers what he has, sincerely wishing to relieve the suffering of others. He happily accepts whatever is offered. When I told this story recently in a Grade 4 classroom, one of the children remarked that it reminded him of the Red Paperclip story, the quirky tale on the blogosphere a few years ago of a young man who set out with a paperclip to "trade up" in the hopes of getting a house. While there were some similarities in the two stories, the principal difference is that the boy in the Indian folktale gives without any thought of return. Only at the end of the story is he asked if there is something he would like to have. By chance, there is and he is bold enough to ask for it.

In the Korean tale "An Ox for a Persimmon" two characters bring gifts to the king, but with very different motivations. Giving with a specific aim in mind is very likely to backfire. We may not get the reward we think we deserve, but if we can connect with the joy of giving, we are guaranteed a reward in the very act of sharing what we have. "A Christmas Doll" is about the pleasure of passing along a precious object, while the Haitian tale "The Chief of the Well" is about hoarding and raises the question of who has control over precious resources. The next story in this section is "Buffalo into Rooster." In this tale from the Indian state of Maharashtra, a series of exchanges leaves a poor farmer with nothing. Surprisingly, his wife does not scold him when he comes home and tells his tale. Generosity is expressed here in both words and actions. Acceptance and love are the best gift of all.

A Drum

HINDI (INDIA)

Indian folktales often reflect the Hindu doctrine of karma, in which human action leads to certain results, depending on the moral quality of the deed. Intention plays an important role in the outcome of any action. An act of kindness or generosity, done without any expectation of return, or reward, will yield a completely different result from one that is performed with the express purpose of getting something back.

A poor woman had only one son. She worked hard cleaning houses and grinding grain for the well-to-do families in town. They gave her some grain in return and she lived on it. But she could never afford to buy nice clothes or toys for her son. Once, when she was going to market with some grain to sell, she asked her son, "What can I bring you from the market?" He promptly replied, "A drum, Mother, get me a drum."

The mother knew she would never have enough money to buy a drum for her son. She went to the market, sold the grain, and bought some gram flour and some salt. She felt sad that she was coming home empty-handed. So when she saw a nice piece of wood on the road, she picked it up and brought it home to her son. The son didn't know what to do with it.

Yet he carried it with him when he went out to play. An old woman was lighting her *chulha*, her woodstove, with some cow-dung patties. The fire was not catching and there was smoke all around and it made the old woman's eyes water. The boy stopped and asked why she was crying. She said that she couldn't light her fire and cook. The boy said, "I have a nice piece of wood and you can start your fire with it." The old

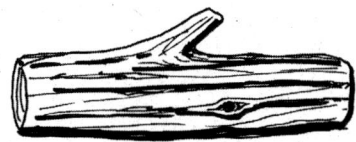

woman was very pleased, lit the fire, made some bread, and gave a piece to the boy.

He took the bread and walked on till he came upon a potter's wife. Her child was crying and flailing his arms. The boy stopped and asked her why the child was crying. The potter's wife said the child was hungry and she had nothing in the house to give him. The boy gave the bread in his hand to the hungry child, who ate it eagerly and stopped crying. The potter's wife was grateful to the boy and gave him a pot.

When he walked on, he came to the river, where he saw a washerman and his wife quarreling. The boy stopped and asked the man why he was scolding and beating his wife. The washerman said, "This woman broke the only pot we had. Now I've nothing to boil my clothes in before I wash them." The boy said, "Here, don't quarrel, take this pot and use it." The washerman was very happy to get a large pot. He gave the boy a coat in return.

The boy walked on. He soon came to a bridge, where he saw a man shivering in the cold without so much as a shirt on him. He asked the man what had happened to his shirt, and the man said, "I was coming to the city on this horse. Robbers attacked me and took everything, even my shirt." The boy said, "Don't worry. You can have this coat." The man took the coat and said, "You're very kind, and I want to give you this horse."

The boy took the horse, and very soon he ran into a wedding party with the musicians, the bridegroom, and his family, but all of them were sitting under a tree with long faces. The boy stopped and asked why they looked so depressed. The bridegroom's father said, "We're all set to go in a wedding procession. But we need a horse for the bridegroom. The man who was supposed to bring it

hasn't arrived. The bridegroom can't arrive on foot. It's getting late, and we'll miss the auspicious hour for the wedding." So the boy offered them his horse, and they were delighted. When the bridegroom asked him what he could do in return, the boy said, "You can give me something: that drum your musician is carrying." The bridegroom had no trouble persuading the drummer to give the drum to the boy. The drummer knew he could easily buy another with the money he was going to get.

The boy now rushed home to his mother, beating his new drum, and told her how he got it, beginning with a piece of wood from the roadside.

Chulha: A traditional clay stove in which wood or dried animal dung are used for fuel.

NOTES

Hindi is one of more than 400 languages spoken in India. "A Drum" was collected from a speaker of this language group.

Hindu is the name we give to a follower of Hinduism, a religion that originally comes from North India but which is now practiced in many countries, including India, Nepal, Sri Lanka, Bangladesh, and Malaysia.

QUESTIONS

৯ *How many gifts do you think were given in this story? Work with a partner and make a list.*

৯ *Have you ever received a gift you didn't know what to do with? What was it?*

৯ *How would you describe the boy in the story? Why does he stop to ask people questions?*

৯ *Which of these gifts might you have kept? Why?*

An Ox for a Persimmon

KOREA

*Gift-giving in Korea, Japan, and other Asian coun-
tries is a traditional way of showing respect, appreciation, and friendship. Offering a gift to a friend
or acquaintance usually obligates that individual
to return the gesture with a gift of slightly greater
value. The person who began the cycle of gift-giving
may then be obliged to present a second, more valuable gift, and so it continues.*

In a certain place there lived two men by the name of Kim and Pak. Mr. Kim was
kind and caring and Mr. Pak was greedy and cunning.

Beside Mr. Kim's house was the stump of a persimmon tree. He watered
it every morning and evening and fertilized it with manure. It grew rapidly into a
strong, healthy tree, and, to everyone's surprise, tiny persimmons appeared on its
branches.

In the autumn, villagers came daily to gaze in wonder at the watermelon-size
persimmons ripening on the tree. When they were finally ripe enough to harvest,
Mr. Kim picked each one with great care and filled many large sacks.

The sight of the bulging sacks filled his heart with joy and he happily shared
the persimmons with his neighbours. Then, thinking the persimmons were truly
unusual, he carefully wrapped up the largest one and set out for Hanyang to deliver
it to the king.

The king stared in disbelief when the royal secretary
placed the persimmon before him. "I've never seen such
a large persimmon. It's magnificent. The man who grew it
deserves an award. Is there anything as big as this among the
gifts I've received lately?"

"Yes, Your Majesty, there is. But, Your Majesty, it is quite
rare and very valuable," said the royal secretary.

"Well, aren't you going to tell me what it is?" exclaimed the King.

"Yes, of course, Your Majesty. It's just . . . that . . . well . . . it is a gold nugget."

"Well, that's no problem. Present it to the man at once."

So it was that Mr. Kim returned home with a gold nugget as big as a watermelon. News of his good fortune spread quickly through the village.

The greedy Mr. Pak was overcome with jealousy and made up his mind to take the king something so that he too would be awarded a gold nugget. He pondered what would be good to take. Finally, he sold all his property in order to purchase an ox and set out for Hanyang with visions of a gold nugget as big as an ox swirling in his head.

"This ox looks like a fine animal. And it's very large," said the king when the royal secretary presented Mr. Pak's gift to him. "I shall give the man who brought it an award. What have I received recently that I can give him?"

"Well, Your Majesty, there is that watermelon-sized persimmon you received a few days ago," replied the royal secretary.

"Oh, yes. That will do nicely," said the king.

Mr. Pak fainted when the royal secretary presented him with the persimmon. And that is how he became a poor man.

※ ❧ ※

GLOSSARY

Persimmon: A sweet, tangy fruit with a soft texture that grows in China and other countries of Asia. It is shaped a bit like a tomato.

QUESTIONS

❧ *Why do people give gifts?*

❧ *What gift-giving traditions do you have in your family?*

❧ *At what time of the year do people give gifts or exchange gifts in different cultures?*

❧ *How does it feel when you give something to someone you love, something you made yourself?*

❧ *How do you think Mr. Kim felt when he was taking the persimmon to the king?*

❧ *What do you think Mr. Pak was thinking about as he led the ox into the king's hall and presented it?*

The Christmas Doll

CANADA

Editor's note: I heard this story from a woman named Phyllis Soles during a workshop I gave on Texada Island on the coast of British Columbia. I had told the "Drum" story, which prompted Phyllis's memory of this experience.

Phyllis loved dolls. She had quite a collection by the time she was eight years old, perhaps a dozen. One of them was an Eaton's Beauty. She stood about two feet tall and had a composition head, as well as composition hands and feet. She even had eyes that opened and shut.

There was a rule in the house that if Phyllis wanted a new doll she would have to give one away. Every year, three weeks before Christmas, a White Gift Service was held at the local United Church in the North End of Halifax where Phyllis and her family lived. Phyllis knew that was when she would bring her gift and lay it on the altar. It wasn't easy for Phyllis to decide which doll to give away. It couldn't be a grubby doll. It had to be one she had taken good care of. A few days before the service, Phyllis would sit down with her dolls all around her. She would think about it and choose one to give away. When she had decided, her mother would wash the doll's clothes and help Phyllis get it ready to give.

On the day of the White Gift Service, Phyllis would walk up the aisle of the church carrying her doll. It was a huge church with three sets of pews. Along the whole front of the church were organ pipes. Phyllis would lay her gift on the platform with the other gifts for the children in need. And when she climbed into the pew with her parents and her brothers, it gave her a good feeling to see her doll sitting there.

The year Phyllis turned eight she wanted a doll that looked like the black children at school. She really liked the black children she went to school with, and she wanted a doll that looked like them. But black dolls were hard to find. She had seen one in a catalogue and that's how she knew they existed, but they weren't in the stores in Halifax. That year her dad was working in New Brunswick and he happened to find a little black doll there. He brought it back when he came home just before Christmas. But in the meantime her mother had found a nice doll in a Halifax store that she planned to give Phyllis. She knew it wasn't what Phyllis had asked for but it was still a new doll. When Phyllis's dad came home with the black doll her parents decided they couldn't give her two dolls. One of them would have to be for another day.

The tradition at Phyllis's house was to be at home for Christmas. The family had a tree that they decorated together. They strung cranberries and draped the strings on the branches. Phyllis and her two brothers would receive a Christmas stocking and one gift each. Christmas morning, as soon as it was light, they took the stockings down from the chimney and brought them into the boys' room to open them together, sitting on her brother's bed. Each stocking would have an apple, an orange, some candy, and a small toy. The candy was called Clear Toy—it was transparent and it came in the shape of an animal, like a donkey or a lamb. Sometimes there was some ribbon candy. It looked like a ribbon wound into a wreath. It was a tan colour.

After breakfast, the children received their gifts. When Phyllis opened hers and saw this very nice doll her mother had bought, she was a little disappointed. Maybe her dad noticed. Anyway, he snuck out the back door and went around through the snow to the front of the house. He took that little black doll—it was only eight inches high—and leaned it up against the front door. Then he knocked and quickly ran back the way he'd come. Phyllis went to open the door and this little doll, dressed in rompers, fell into the hall. Phyllis squealed in delight she was so happy.

Postscript

Phyllis remembers: "I kept that doll for years and years. It always made me think of my dad and what a wonderful man he was. All the children on our street loved him. We had the only car on the block and in the summer when he was home he would load it up with kids and take us all to the beach. It turns out the doll was the last thing my dad ever gave me, because he died after Christmas dinner that same day. He lay down on the couch and he never got up. That story about the boy who asked for a drum made me think of that doll and my dad."

❄ ❄ ❄

Eaton's Beauty: The first Eaton Beauty doll was introduced in 1900. The smallest dolls cost a dollar, which was quite a bit of money in those days—the equivalent of $27 in 2012. For the first five or six years, the bisque heads were shoulderheads (the head and shoulder plate were all one piece) with sleep eyes and curly mohair wigs. The bodies were made of kid leather and were jointed at the knees, hips, elbows, and shoulders. Bisque heads were made of unglazed china. "Composition" bodies were made from a paste of fine sawdust, cornstarch and glue. Each company had their own formula.

White Gift Service: The tradition of the White Gift Service began in the Methodist Church early in the twentieth century. At that time, Christian communities held gift exchanges in celebration of Christmas. They realized that some members of the church could not bring extravagant gifts, and that some who received fine gifts already had more than they needed. They found help in the tale of Kublai Khan, who received gifts from his subjects only if they were wrapped in plain white paper. No comparisons were allowed, and all gifts were accepted gladly. A new Christian tradition was born! Gifts would be brought anonymously and distributed to those who needed them and would most appreciate them, as an act of worship.

QUESTIONS

§ *Why do you think Phyllis's parents had a rule that if she wanted a new doll she had to give one away?*

§ *How do you think Phyllis decided which doll to give away?*

§ *Why was the little black doll special to Phyllis?*

The Chief of the Well

In Haiti the storyteller begins her performance by calling out "Kric!" To show they are ready the members of the audience call out "Krac!" in reply. Now the storytelling can begin. The children and adults can expect songs, chants, and even dances, as part of the story.

There was once a drought in the country. The streams dried up and the wells went dry. There was no place for anybody to get water. The animals met to discuss the situation—the cow, the dog, the goat, the horse, the donkey, and all the others. They decided to ask God for help. Together they went to God and told him how bad things were.

God thought, then he said, "Don't bother your heads. They don't call me God for nothing. I will give you one well for everyone to use."

The animals thanked God. They told him he was very considerate. God said, "But you'll have to take good care of my well. One of you will have to be caretaker. He will stay by the well at all times to see that no one abuses it or makes it dirty."

Mabouya, the ground lizard, spoke up saying, "I will be caretaker."

God looked at all the animals. He said at last, "Mabouya, the lizard, looks like the best caretaker. Therefore, I appoint him. He will be the watchman. The well is over there in the mango grove."

The animals went away. The lizard went directly to the well. When the other animals began to come back for water, Mabouya challenged them. First the cow came to drink. The lizard sang out in a deep voice:

"*Qui est là?* Who's there? *Qui est là?* Who's there?

Who is walking in my grove?"

The cow replied:

"*C'est moi, la vache.* It is I, the cow.

I am coming for water. *J'ai soif.*"

And the lizard called back:

"*Va t-en!* Go away! This is God's grove,

And the well is dry."

So the cow went away and suffered from thirst.

When the horse came the lizard challenged him, saying:

"*Qui est là?* Who's there? *Qui est là?* Who's there?

Who is walking in my grove?"

The horse answered:

"*C'est moi, le cheval.* It is I, the horse.

I am coming for water. *J'ai soif.*"

And the lizard called back:

"*Va-t-en!* Go away! This is God's grove,

And the well is dry."

So the horse went away and he too suffered from thirst.

Each animal came to the well and the lizard challenged all of them in the same way, saying:

"*Va-t-en!* Go away! This is God's grove,

And the well is dry."

So the animals went away and suffered much because they had no water to drink.

When God saw all the suffering going on, he said, "I gave the animals a well to drink from, but they are all dying of thirst. What is the matter? *Qu'est-ce qui se passe?*" And he himself went to the well. When the lizard heard God's footsteps, he called out:

"*Qui est là?* Who's there? *Qui est là?* Who's there?

Who is walking in my grove?"

God answered:

"*C'est moi, Papa Dieu.* It is I, Papa God.

I am coming for water. *J'ai soif.*"

And the lizard said:

"*Va-t-en, Papa Dieu.* Go away, Papa God.

The well is dry."

God was very angry. He said once more:

"*C'est moi, Papa Dieu.* It is I, Papa God.

I am coming for water. *J'ai soif.*"

And the lizard called back to him again:

"*Va-t-en, Papa Dieu.* Go away, Papa God.

The well is dry."

God spoke no more to the lizard. He sent for the animals to come to the well. He said, "You came to me because you were thirsty and I gave you a well. I made Mabouya the caretaker. But he gave no thought to the suffering creatures all around him. If a man has a banana tree in his garden, it is his. But if a man has a well in his garden, only the hole in the ground belongs to him. The water is God's and belongs to all the creatures. Because Mabouya, the lizard, became drunk with conceit, he is no longer the caretaker. From now on, he must drink his water from puddles wherever the rain falls. The new caretaker will be the frog. The frog will not say, 'Go away, the well is dry.' She will say, 'This is God's well; this is God's well'."

So the animals drank at the well, while Mabouya, the lizard went away from it and drank rainwater wherever he could find it. The frog is now the caretaker. And all night she calls out:

"This is God's well! *Venez boire.*

This is God's well! *Venez boire.*"

And it is a saying among the people:

"The hole in the ground is yours,

But the water is God's and belongs to all the creatures."

❧ ❧ ❧

GLOSSARY

Pronunciation of French words:

Qui est là? Key ay la?

C'est moi, la vache. Say mwah, la vash.

J'ai soif. Geay swahf.

Va t-en! Va ton *(don't pronounce the "n")*.

C'est moi, le cheval. Say mwah, leuh sheval.

C'est moi, Papa Dieu. Say mwah, Papa Deeyeuh.

Venez boire. Veuhnay bwahre.

QUESTIONS

❧ *What is the job of a caretaker?*

❧ *What kinds of things do you take care of?*

❧ *Why do you think Mabouya offers to be the caretaker of the well?*

❧ *Why do you think God appoints Mabouya?*

❧ *Why do the animals believe Mabouya when he says there is no water in the well?*

❧ *Do you think Frog will be a good caretaker?*

Buffalo into Rooster

MARATHI

Miracles appear in many Marathi folktales. Here gods, goddesses, and fairies often help the poor and the miserable. Even demons are sometimes kind.

It is not easy to come across an affectionate and devoted couple like Patil and his wife Janai. With a little property, they led a contented life with their children in a small village. Everyone knew them as kind-hearted and generous.

One day Patil's wife said to him, "Since we are getting older, why don't we sell one of the buffaloes? One animal will be enough for us and less work."

"Very well," said Patil. "I will take it to the market tomorrow."

The next day Patil set out early in the morning for the market. Along the way, he met a man with a horse who said, "Where are you going at such an early hour?"

"To the market, to sell this old buffalo."

The buffalo looked to be a fine animal. The man seemed to take a fancy to it. He said, "Why go all the way to the market? If you like my horse I'll exchange it for your buffalo."

Patil gave it some thought. If he couldn't sell the horse it would be fun for the children to have a horse to ride. He said, "Very well. Give me your horse and you take the buffalo."

He mounted the horse and continued on his way, but after a few paces he realized the horse was blind. Next he met a man with a cow.

"Where are you going with that horse?" asked the man.

"I was on my way to the market to sell my old buffalo. But I exchanged it for this horse and it turns out the horse is blind."

"Exchanged your buffalo for a blind horse? Why don't you take my cow? She's a fine animal."

Patil thought the cow did look like a fine animal. Moreover, he thought to himself, if he couldn't sell it, it would be less work than the horse. So he took the cow for the horse and went on his way, but he soon discovered the cow was lame in one leg.

Next he met a man with a she-goat.

"Where are you going with that cow?" asked the man.

"I started in the morning to sell my old buffalo which I exchanged for a blind horse. Now I have got this lame cow for the horse. I am going to sell it, if I can."

"Sell it?" said the man. "Why, my she-goat is much better than your lame cow. If you like it, you can have it for your cow."

Patil took the she-goat. He soon found that it was ill. On the last part of the journey he met a man with a rooster. After a brief conversation, he exchanged the goat for the rooster.

When he reached the market, it was midday. Patil was hungry but he had no money with him. He had planned to buy some supplies with the money from the sale of the buffalo. But now all he had was a rooster.

With great difficulty he was able to sell the rooster for one rupee. This was enough to buy some food to eat. After washing his hands and feet, he sat down under a pipal tree, with his meal on a leaf. But before he could eat a single morsel, a man in ragged clothes appeared before him and said in a pleading tone, "Give a poor man some food. I have not eaten anything in two days and I am dying of hunger. God will bless you." When Patil saw the poor man's condition, he gave him all the food he had and started for home.

Meanwhile, Patil's wife had scrubbed the house neat and clean and cooked the meal for the whole family. After completing her work, she was sitting in the backyard telling stories to her children, waiting for her husband's return. When Patil got home, he sat himself down to rest.

His wife was eager for his news. "I have been waiting for you!" she said.

"Please bring me a cup of water and I will tell you what happened today."

After drinking the water, Patil said: "I did not sell the buffalo. I exchanged it for a horse."

"Is that so? That's wonderful!" said his wife. "The children will have so much fun riding a horse. Who needs a buffalo? Run along, children. Go and tie the horse up."

"Wait, wait!" said Patil. "I don't have the horse anymore. I exchanged it for a cow."

"Even better," said his wife. "A cow is more useful than a horse, and now the children will get plenty of cow's milk. Go along, children! Bring in the cow."

"No, wait. I would have brought the cow home, but I exchanged it for a she-goat."

"Very good," said his wife. "Goat's milk is said to have medicinal properties. And goats look after themselves. Let's go and see the goat."

"But, listen. I exchanged the she-goat for a rooster."

"Well, that's just what we need. The rooster will wake us up early in the morning. Children, take the rooster into the yard."

"Wait! I haven't finished. I had the rooster, but I was very hungry and I sold it for a rupee to buy some food."

"Fine, very fine," said his wife. "But did you have enough food to eat? Why do we need a rooster? What matters is your well-being and happiness."

"But you must hear the rest. I gave all my food to an old man who came begging."

"And you remained hungry? Oh well. It doesn't matter. Indeed, it was a kind act. Never turn away a beggar when he comes at mealtime. Now get up, wash your feet and come for your meal. I have been missing you all day."

They had a good meal and went to bed. Early the next morning when Patil got up and opened the door, he was very surprised by what he saw. He called his wife. In front of the door stood a buffalo that was not old, a horse that was not blind, a cow that was not lame, a she-goat in good health, and a fine-looking rooster. Beside the animals, there was a leaf with a shining rupee in the middle of it. They were amazed.

Patil's wife whispered, "Do you know who could have done this? The beggar you fed yesterday, that must have been . . .

"None other than God," said Patil.

❧ ❧ ❧

GLOSSARY

Marathi: The official language of Maharashtra, the third most populated state of India.

QUESTIONS

❧ *How do you think Patil felt when he discovered he had exchanged a healthy buffalo for a blind horse?*

❧ *Patil has bad luck, but still he gives away his meal. What makes him capable of generosity when he himself is in need?*

❧ *How do we know that Patil's wife loved him?*

How the Kangaroo Got Her Pouch

In the culture of the Aborigines of Australia all of life is kin. Kinship binds the members of the community, not only to each other, but also to the stars, the earth, the plants, the animals, the very rocks and landscape. To the Aboriginal person, the entire universe is permeated with life—it is a living, breathing, biomass which has separated into families. There are families of stars, of trees and of animals, and these are connected to our human families.

Long ago the kangaroo was grooming her joey on the bank of a brook. They liked to listen to the water burble as the mama combed her baby's fur. On this day, an old wombat staggered toward them.

"Oh dear," the kangaroo whispered to her baby. "This wombat is old and sick. He must have great-great-grandchildren already."

The mother kangaroo thought she heard the sound of weeping. As the wombat veered closer, she heard him say, "Useless and worthless, worthless and useless."

"What's the trouble, friend wombat?" she asked.

"Huh?" he said, startled. "Who said that? Did somebody speak?"

"I did," said the kangaroo. "It's a mother kangaroo and her joey."

"I'm blind," the wombat replied. "Nobody wants me around. Nobody thinks about me. I'm no good any more. They've abandoned me, all of them."

The kangaroo, who had a tender heart, said, "It's not as bad as all that. I'll be your friend. My joey and I will show you where the tastiest grass grows." She turned around and let the wombat hold on to her strong tail. Then, slowly, she led him over to the juiciest grass and cleanest water. The old wombat sighed with pleasure. It made the kangaroo happy to see him feeling better.

Suddenly she remembered her joey! She had told him to stay close, but he had wandered off again. She raced back to look for him. So many times this had happened. She'd have her head down pulling up grass, and when she looked up, he had wandered off. It scared her terribly.

She found her joey asleep under a gum tree. Not wanting to wake him from his nap, she decided to go back and check on the old wombat. Something was moving in the bush. An Aborignal hunter, silently stalking the wombat! Already his boomerang was raised above his head, its smooth edges ready to slice the air. The kangaroo froze. She couldn't even breathe. She wanted to run, but the wombat was like her joey—she had to protect him!

The kangaroo began to stomp on the branches and twigs under her feet. Thump, thump, crack, crack, she pounded the earth. The hunter turned toward her. "Run!" she screamed to the wombat, "Run! There's a hunter." The wombat took off crazily, not knowing where he was going. The hunter didn't care. Now all he wanted was the kangaroo!

She hopped as hard and fast as she could into the bush, away, away from where she had left her joey asleep. Her heart thumped wildly in her throat as she ran for her life. At last she came to a cave. She was too tired to go farther, and collapsed on the dirt floor inside. At least he would have to kill her in the cool dark, not out in the open where other animals would be forced to watch.

The hunter ran past the mouth of the cave! The kangaroo stayed inside, listening for his return. She was afraid to go out. Finally, she saw him walk past the mouth of the cave again, his boomerang hanging from his hand. She waited until it was safe, then ran as fast as she could back to the gum tree. There was her joey, awake and ready to play. Together they went to look for the wombat, but he had gone.

What the kangaroo mother didn't know was that the wombat wasn't a wombat. He was actually the great god Byamee who had put on a disguise. Byamee had descended from the sky world to find out which of his creatures had the kindest heart. Now he had an answer that pleased him greatly: the kangaroo. Byamee wanted to give her the gift that would help her most of all. So he called the sky spirits together and said, "Go down below to where the eucalyptus grow tall. Peel the long strips of bark and make a dilly bag apron. Give it to the kangaroo mother and explain that she must tie it around her waist."

And so they did. At the very moment the kangaroo mother tied the apron around her waist, Byamee transformed it into soft kangaroo fur. It grew into her own flesh. Now she had a pouch in which to carry her baby joey. He could even sleep in there as she went about her daily tasks.

The kangaroo mother was very happy with her gift. But because she was the kindest creature of all, she didn't want to keep it only for herself. She thought about the other kangaroo mothers and about the wallaby mothers and the kangaroo rats and all the other marsupials.

Byamee loved the kangaroo's generous heart. So he decided to make pouches for all the other marsupial mothers. Ever since then, their babies almost never get lost.

𝕏 𝕍 𝕏

GLOSSARY

Joey: A young kangaroo or wallaby.

Dilly bag apron: A bag made of strips of bark or plaited grass for carrying food

QUESTIONS

𝑆 *How does Byamee find out about the kangaroo's generous heart?*

𝑆 *How did the kangaroo feel when her joey wandered off?*

𝑆 *Where do we see the kangaroo's generous heart?*

𝑆 *Do you know anyone who is like the mother kangaroo?*

FIVE

THE GIFT OF FRIENDSHIP

Hold a true friend with both your hands.

—NIGERIAN PROVERB

What *a gift it is to have a friend.* In the first friendships we form we discover the pleasure of sharing experience. Together we encounter the thrill of physical challenges, the mysterious and fascinating world of bugs and the living environment around us. We learn that sharing what we treasure increases our happiness. We also discover that difference is to be valued and appreciated.

Over many years of telling "The Antelope, the Woodpecker, and the Turtle," I have asked countless children and adults to tell me what it means to be a friend or to have one. "A friend knows you," said one Grade 5 student. Truly, this itself is an amazing gift. To be known is to be seen and accepted in our unique imperfection. To be known is to be connected. When I repeated this bit of wisdom to a group of adults, one of them added, "Yes. A friend knows you, *and* she lets herself be known." In other words, a friend does not hide her vulnerability, her fears, and anxieties. In the Cherokee story of the bird named Meadowlark, we see a beautiful example of this aspect of friendship. When Grasshopper comes upon Meadowlark hiding in the grass and asks him why, he tells the truth. He is ashamed of his big feet. By sharing his embarrassment and shame, Meadowlark allows Grasshopper to give him some direct advice and encouragement. And later, knowing about Meadowlark's big feet is what permits Grasshopper to link Meadowlark and Quail, whose eggs are in danger of being crushed.

Friendship has its shadow side, as we all know from painful memories of being teased or taunted by those who know our weaknesses. The Haitian story "The King of the Animals" reminds us of the importance of celebrating each other's strengths. Here we see in humorous detail how easy it is to discount each other's abilities by focusing on perceived shortcomings. Friendship invites us to enlarge our perception, reaching out to include those whom we perceive as not "our kind." In the Korean folktale, "The Value of Salt," a salt-seller and his wife use the medium of food to teach their son-in-law's parents to value and respect their daughter, even though she is from a different class.

In the final story in this chapter we see how the gift of friendship has an impact beyond the relationship itself. "The Friendship Orchard" tells of two friends who argue over a box of gold that has been unearthed in their fields. Each stubbornly insists that the other one should take it. The wise man to whom they go for advice gives them some simple advice—to use the treasure for the benefit of others by planting an orchard of fruit trees. The trees are an apt metaphor for the potential legacy of friendship—that it can be a gift to future generations, providing beauty, shade, and nourishment.

The Antelope, the Woodpecker, and the Turtle

INDIA

In the Buddhist tradition, there is a collection of stories called the Jataka. These are said to be the Buddha's own memories of his former lives. In each story the Buddha is seen developing qualities such as loving-kindness, generosity, patience, and equanimity.

Once, in the past, the Buddha-to-be was born as an antelope. Kurunga-miga was his name. He lived in a thicket in the middle of the woods, by a lake. At the top of a tree by that very same lake there lived a woodpecker—*Satapatto*. And in the lake, there lived a turtle—*Kacchapo*. The antelope, the woodpecker, and the turtle were friends. They lived together and they took care of each other.

How did they take care of each other? Well, they told each other stories.

The woodpecker's stories were short, and to the point. They went like this: "Da, da-da. Da, da-da, da, da." The turtle's stories, on the other hand, were slow and ponderous. They went on and on, and on, until sometimes, the woodpecker and the antelope fell asleep. The stories told by the antelope, on the other hand, spoke of things he had seen in the forest—creatures living their lives, teaching their young how to be in the world. Somehow, whenever the antelope told one of his stories, the woodpecker and the turtle felt a little kinder, and a little wiser.

One day a hunter entered the forest. He happened to see the hoof-prints of the antelope in the soft earth by the edge of the lake, where Kurunga-miga went to drink each night. The hunter laid a snare. It was made of leather, but it was strong as an iron chain. Then he went away. That night, when Kurunga-miga came to drink, his leg was caught in the snare. He cried out in fear.

Down from the top of the tree flew Satapatto, the woodpecker. Out from the water of the lake climbed Kacchapo, the turtle. They looked and saw their friend the antelope, with his hind-leg trapped in the snare, trembling and frightened.

"What can we do?" said Kacchapo, his wet shell gleaming in the moonlight.

"I know," said Satapatto. "You have a beak, Kacchapo. Use your beak. Chew and cut this leather snare. I will fly through the woods to the hunter's lodge. I will slow the hunter and prevent him from coming at first light."

Kacchapo sat down and began to cut and chew the snare.

Khadati, khadati, khadati.

Khadati, khadati, khadati.

As he chewed Kurunga-miga, the antelope, murmured the turtle's name to encourage him.

He said, "*Kacchapo. Kacchapo. Kacchapo.*"

Meanwhile the woodpecker flew through the woods. The sound of his wings lifting and falling made a sound, like the sound of his own name:

Satapatto, Satapatto, Satapatto.

Satapatto, Satapatto, Satapatto.

He flew through the forest, right to the hunter's lodge. There he alighted in a  tree, and waited for any sound of the hunter preparing to set out. When light first showed in the east he heard the hunter moving about. Inside the lodge, the hunter slung his leather pouch over one shoulder. He took his knife in one hand. Then he opened the door. At that very moment Satapatto cried out, flew down from the tree, flapped his wings, and struck the hunter in the face. The hunter was amazed. "What is this bird of evil omen?" He turned about and shut the door. He unslung his leather pouch and set it down. He put down his knife, and lay down on his bed. This was not a good way to start the day.

The hunter said to himself, "This bird struck me in the face when I went through the front door. Now I'll go by the back door."

But Satapatto, waiting in the tree, thought to himself, "This hunter came out by the front door. The second time he'll go by the back door."

Satapatto flew to the rear of the hunter's lodge. He alighted in a tree and waited. When the hunter opened the door and stepped out Satapatto flew down from the tree, flapped his wings, and struck the hunter in the face.

The hunter was astonished. "This bird does not want me to set out!"

He turned about and shut the door.

Now he waited until the sun began to climb over the treetops, into the sky.

Then he took up his knife and his pouch and opened the door. Crouching low, he went quickly along the forest trails towards the lake.

Satapatto flew ahead of him to warn the antelope and the turtle. His wings went up and down, even more quickly than before.

Satapatto, Satapatto, Satapatto.
Satapatto, Satapatto, Satapatto.

He flew through the woods to the edge of the lake, where Kurunga-miga, the antelope, was caught in the hunter's snare.

"The hunter is coming! The hunter is coming!" warned the woodpecker.

All night long the turtle had cut and chewed the snare. His beak was broken. There was blood at the edges of his mouth. He was weak and exhausted. But only one thin strand of the leather snare remained.

"The hunter is coming!" warned Satapatto.

Kurunga-miga looked and saw the hunter coming with his knife. He snapped the leather snare and went running down the trail. The woodpecker flew up into a tree, and when the hunter arrived, there was no antelope in his snare, but there, at the edge of the lake, was a beautiful turtle, with a beautiful turtle shell. He picked up Kacchapo and put him in his leather pouch.

As he ran down the trail, Kurunga-miga looked back. He saw that his friend Kacchapo had been seized. He said to himself, "I will save my friend." He came back a little ways on the trail. He pretended to stumble. He made sure that the hunter could see him.

The hunter did see him. "This little antelope is weak," he said. "I will catch him easily." He unslung the leather pouch and set it on the ground. Then he set off after the antelope.

Kurunga-miga led the hunter this way and that way on the forest trails, never letting him come too close, but never letting him stray too far behind. He led him right to the other side of the lake. Then he summoned all his strength and came leaping and jumping, swift as the wind, right back to the spot where Kacchapo was trapped in the leather pouch. He crouched down low and caught the pouch on his two sharp, pointed horns. He lifted it up and let it fall. The pouch split open, and out stepped Kacchapo. Then down from the tree flew Satapatto and alighted on the ground.

Kurunga-miga spoke to the turtle and the woodpecker: "My friends," he said, "Kacchapo, Satapatto. You have done for me what ought to be done by a friend. You have given me my life. Now, quickly, before the hunter returns, Satapatto, take your young ones and fly through the woods to safety. And you, Kacchapo, hide yourself in the waters of the lake, where the hunter will not see you. And I will run and hide in the thicket."

They each went their separate ways, and when the hunter came back he found only a broken snare and a torn pouch. He looked closely and saw the hoof-prints of the antelope, drops of blood from the turtle's beak, and one black wing-feather. There, on the forest floor, he read the story of their friendship.

"This feather, could it be from the bird that struck me in the face this very morning?" he asked himself. "And this snare, see how it has been cut and chewed. Could it be that the turtle used his sharp beak to cut the snare and release the antelope? And these hoof-prints returning . . . did the antelope come back to rescue the turtle?"

He was amazed, and shaking his head in disbelief, he gathered up the torn pouch and the broken snare. He set off, disappointed and discouraged, but hoping that next time he might catch some creatures who didn't have such good friends.

🐜 🐢 🦌

QUESTIONS

§ *How do you think the three creatures became friends?*

§ *How did they help each other in this story?*

The Bird that was Ashamed of it Feet

CHEROKEE

This is what the old people told me when I was a child, about the days when the world was new and all creatures still spoke the same language. Now, in those days, there was a bird called Meadowlark, whose feet grew so big he was ashamed of them. While the other birds flew through the air and sang in the treetops, Meadowlark hid himself in the tall grass where no one could see him. He spent all his time staring down at his feet and worrying about them.

"Provider must have made a terrible mistake," thought Meadowlark, turning his feet this way and that. No matter how he looked at them, all Meadowlark could see was how big his feet were. "Perhaps Creator thought this would be a funny joke to play," said Meadowlark. "I'm sure anyone who saw my big feet would laugh at them, but I do not think this is funny at all." And so Meadowlark continued to hide himself in the tall grass.

One day Grasshopper was going about his business, making his way through the tall grass, when he bumped smack into Meadowlark, sitting on the ground and staring sadly at his feet.

"What are you doing here?" asked Grasshopper. "You are not one of those birds who live on the ground! You should be in the treetops with the other birds. Why do you not fly and sing as they do?"

"I am ashamed," answered Meadowlark. "These feet that Provider gave me are so big and ugly that I am afraid that everyone will laugh at me!"

Grasshopper looked down at Meadowlark's feet, and his eyes grew big with amazement. It was true; Meadowlark's feet were huge! Grasshopper did his best not to smile; he did not want to hurt Meadowlark's feelings.

Finally he said, "Well, it is true that your feet are perhaps a bit larger than those of other birds your size. But Creator does not make mistakes. If your feet are big, you may be sure they will be useful to you someday. Big feet will not keep you from flying. Big feet will not stop

you from singing. You are a bird and you should act like one!" And Grasshopper went on about his business.

After Grasshopper had gone on his way, Meadowlark sat and thought about his words. "Perhaps he is right," said Meadowlark. "The size of my feet cannot change the sound of my voice or the power of my wings. I should use the gifts Creator gave me." And so Meadowlark took Grasshopper's advice and flew out to sing. He landed in the top of a tree, threw back his head, and let his song pour from his throat. Meadowlark could really sing! Piercingly sweet and beautiful, the liquid notes of Meadowlark's song spread through the forest.

One by one, the animal people stopped what they were doing and gathered to listen to Meadowlark's voice. Raccoon, Possum, and Skunk; Deer, Bear, and Wolf; even Rabbit paused in his scurrying about to listen in wonder to this marvelous singer. The other birds flocked around Meadowlark, listening. Even Mockingbird fell silent, entranced by the melody that Meadowlark sang.

When Meadowlark began to sing, he forgot everything else, even his big feet. He closed his eyes and lost himself in the joyful song Creator had given him. When at last he finished his song and looked around, there were all the other birds and animals, staring at him. With a rush of shame, Meadowlark remembered his feet. Thinking that the others were staring at him because he was so ugly, Meadowlark flew back down to the tall grass and hid. and this time he would not come out.

Not very far from the tall grass where Meadowlark hid, there was a wheat field planted by the Human Beings. Now there was a Quail who had made her nest and laid her eggs in the middle of this wheat field. Every day she sat on her nest and waited for her eggs to hatch. As the wheat grew ripe and her eggs had still not hatched, Quail began to worry. Sure enough, one afternoon she heard the people talking about how they were going to come out and cut the wheat the very next day. Quail knew that her nest would be trampled and her eggs crushed, and she began to cry.

Now Grasshopper heard Quail crying, and he came to see what was wrong. "The men are coming to cut the wheat," Quail cried, "and my family will die!"

Suddenly Grasshopper had an idea. "Wait here," he told Quail. "I think I know someone who can help."

Grasshopper hurried to find Meadowlark. "Quail needs help to move her family," said Grasshopper, "and I think your big feet are the answer."

When Meadowlark heard of Quail's trouble, he agreed at once to try to help. He flew to Quail's nest. There he found that his big feet were just the right size to pick up Quail's eggs. Very carefully, Meadowlark lifted Quail's eggs and flew with them to the safety of the tall grass. There Quail built a new nest, and it was not long before the eggs hatched. As Meadowlark watched Quail tending her beautiful babies, he thought to himself, "My feet may be big and ugly, but they did a good thing. I should not be ashamed of them!"

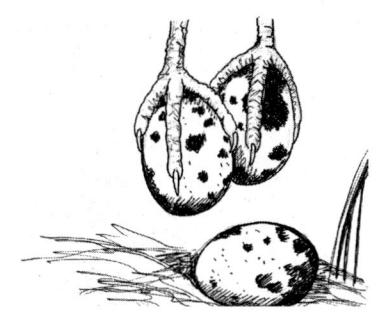

And so Meadowlark flew out of the tall grass, back to the treetops where he began to sing. He is singing to this day, and his song is still so beautiful that everyone stops to listen.

※ ❦ ☙

QUESTIONS

❧ *Where is there generosity in this story?*

❧ *How does Grasshopper show his friendship to Meadowlark?*

❧ *What happens when Meadowlark agrees to help Quail?*

The King of the Animals

HAITI

In Haiti more than half of the population can neither read nor write. As a result, wisdom is oral. People express their knowledge and hand it down in proverbs. In the rural parts of the country, when a serious conversation is underway, it is only a matter of time before someone quotes a proverb in support of an idea. There are hundreds of proverbs. One very famous one is:

Piti, piti, wazo fe nich li.
Little by little the bird builds its nest

Once upon a time the animals decided they needed a king.

A gathering was called. Drummers marched from one village to another to announce the event.

"Come and choose a king.

Venez choisir un roi.

Let us have a king or queen.

Venez élire une reine."

The message was carried in every direction. Preparations began. A large court was made ready for dancing and celebration. Food was cooked—lots of it. And the animals came.

There was a tremendous crowd. The tree lizard, Zandolite, was the chairman. He addressed the gathering:

"Brothers and sisters," he said, "we need a king, or a queen. In the old days, we had a king and sometimes we had a queen, and in those times everything was in good order. Nowadays, when we have no king and no queen, there is much disorder. Every man is for himself, and there is trouble all around. Let us select our leader."

There was noisy discussion among the animals. Then someone called out,

"Let the bull be our king."

"*Le taureau, le taureau!*" The bull stepped forward. He snorted and stamped his feet. He was very proud.

How handsome and strong he looked. He swung his head from one side to the other so that everyone could see his horns. The animals talked among themselves, and at last they said,

"No, the bull isn't fit to be king. He is strong, but he likes to fight. He puts his head down and threatens anyone who stands in his way."

Then someone said, "Let the nanny-goat be queen."

"*Oui, le chèvre! Le chèvre!*"

"She's persistent. When she wants something, she goes after it."

The nanny-goat stepped forward, her white coat gleaming in the sun. Just then, she noticed a bush nearby. She didn't think anyone would notice if she had a nibble.

The animals discussed the question again, and after a while the crowd said, "No, the nanny-goat isn't fit to be queen. She eats the leaves off the coffee plants. She stands around for hours munching, with her beard bobbing up and down. Who wants a queen who is always eating?"

"Let us consider the rabbit," someone said. "The rabbit is kind. He's gentle."

"*Le lapin?* The rabbit? Whenever someone comes along, the rabbit has to jump out of the way. He hides in the grass. And he twitches his nose. He has no dignity."

"Well, then let the she-donkey be queen," someone suggested.

"*Oui. L'ânesse. Pourquoi pas?* She works hard. She's steady."

"What!" the people said in disgust. "The donkey? Should we have for a queen a person who carries coffee and charcoal on her back all day? What would people think of us? We need a leader of whom we can be proud."

"Well, then, let the snake be king. He's flexible."

"*Le serpent!* The snake?" the crowd answered. "The person who lives in a hole in the ground? If you step on him, he wriggles but never makes a sound of protest. He crawls on his belly. No, he can't be king."

"What about the horse?" someone said.

"*Oui! Le cheval!*"

"The horse? How could we have as king a person with a bit in his mouth and a man on his back? No, no, not the horse."

Each animal whose name came up was rejected for this reason or that.

At last only the dog was left.

"Let the dog be king," someone called out.

"*Le chien! Le chien!*"

There was applause. The animals said, "Yes, let us make the dog our leader."

They crowded around him. They started the ceremony to make the dog the king of the animals. The drums were drumming. Flags were waving. The food was cooking. As they dressed the dog in his royal clothes, he smelled the meat cooking over the fire nearby. It made him very hungry. His mouth watered. They wiped his face. Saliva ran out of his mouth. They wiped his face again. Suddenly, because he couldn't control himself any longer, the dog broke loose, seized the meat in his teeth, and ran away.

"Our king is gone!" everyone shouted.

Then they began to say, "No, he isn't our king. He has stolen the meat. He is a thief. How could we have a thief for our king?"

So the great gathering broke up. Everyone went home.

This is the way it was: all of the creatures who were put forward for king or queen were rejected because they were judged by their weaknesses. Had they been considered according to their strong points rather than their weaknesses, the animals would now have a king or a queen. As it is, they do not.

⚜ ⚜ ⚜

QUESTIONS

ß *What do you think makes a good leader?*

ß *Why is it difficult for the animals to choose one?*

The Value of Salt

Salt is the main ingredient in Korean cooking. Korean food revolves around the following six ingredients: soybean paste, soy sauce, red pepper paste, Kimc'i, salted seafood and salt. Of these six, salt is the foundation of the other five.

A long, long time ago the son of a wealthy man fell in love with the daughter of a salt peddler. However, his parents would not hear of his marrying her because at that time society was strictly segregated into classes according to occupation and peddling salt was among the lowest.

To his parents' great embarrassment, the young man stubbornly refused any marriage they tried to arrange, saying he would not marry if he could not marry the daughter of the salt peddler. He was so adamant that his parents finally consented and the two were married.

However, the girl was constantly abused by her in-laws. Despite her husband's constant protests, they called her names and made snide remarks about her appearance. But, even though she wept inwardly, she never complained, not even to her husband, and diligently went about her daily chores.

Her parents were very sad to learn how she was treated. One day her mother said to her father, "I wish there was something we could do to make life better for her. I can't eat or sleep for thinking about how unhappy she must be living in that house where everyone looks down on her. There must be something we could do . . . "

"I have an idea," she said after a while. "Let's invite her parents-in-law to dinner."

"Do you really think they would come?" chortled the salt peddler.

"If we insist, I think they will. But we must insist. And this is what I plan to do . . . " she explained.

"Well, let's give it a try," agreed the salt peddler.

The in-laws laughed when they received the dinner invitation and flatly refused. But the salt peddler and his wife were so insistent that they finally agreed.

The salt peddler and his wife humbly welcomed the in-laws into their home. As was the custom, the salt peddler and the father-in-law sat down to drink. The salt peddler poured the father-in-law a cup of wine and the father-in-law filled the salt peddler's cup and they drank. Of course, after a drink, the father-in-law ate one of the delicacies the salt peddler's wife had prepared for *anju*. He could not believe how strange it tasted. It was so bland he could not eat another bite.

Meanwhile, the wife placed a table of food in front of the mother-in-law. The mother-in-law ate some rice and then ate a morsel from one of the side dishes. It was bland. She ate a spoonful of soup. It was also tasteless. She ate a piece of *kimc'i*. It too was tasteless. It seemed that none of the food was seasoned. She put down her spoon and chopsticks, indicating that she was finished eating.

"Please eat some more," said the salt peddler's wife. "You've hardly eaten a bite."

"Oh, I can't. I'm still full from breakfast," said the mother-in-law.

"Here, have another drink," said the salt peddler, extending his empty cup to the father-in-law.

"Oh, no, no," said the father-in-law. "I can't eat another bite so there's no way I can drink."

"Well, I have something to say," said the salt peddler, and he took a deep breath. "I know that you are not eating because the food is tasteless. It is tasteless because it doesn't have a single grain of salt in it. My wife deliberately made it that way to show you how indispensable salt is to our diet. As you have just experienced, it is difficult to eat without it. The King must have salt. Wealthy people like you must have salt. Even a beggar must have salt. Everyone must have salt to make food palatable. And there must be someone to make it available for them. Just as there must be farmers, there must be merchants and there must be rulers. If everyone had a choice, do you think there would be any farmers? Or salt peddlers? Or butchers? What kind of world would it be without them? And what kind of world would it be without salt? I know that I am speaking out of place, but I wanted to explain to you the value of salt and ask you to love my daughter."

The parents-in-law stood up and bowed low to the salt peddler and his wife. "You're absolutely right. No matter how wealthy a person is, he can't live without salt," said the father-in-law in a humble voice. "And thank you for showing me that we all need each other to get along in this world."

And from that time on the wealthy family and the salt peddler's family visited back and forth often and the wealthy couple loved their daughter-in-law and had only words of praise for her.

✳ ✳ ✳

Anju*:* A general term for Korean side dishes consumed while drinking alcohol

Kimc'i *(*pronounced *kimchee):* A traditional Korean dish made of fermented vegetables, flavoured with a variety of seasonings

QUESTIONS

❦ *Why do the wealthy couple look down on the salt peddler's daughter?*

❦ *How do the salt peddler and his wife teach them a lesson?*

❦ *What is that lesson?*

The Friendship Orchard

CENTRAL ASIA—KAZAKHSTAN

Two elderly friends tilled a small patch of earth on the barren steppe. They raised vegetables and a few sheep, but life was hard and they earned little. Winter was especially difficult because of the dreaded snowstorms known as *dzhut*, in which previously thawed snow froze over. Sheep couldn't dig though the ice for food and often perished. Because they were old and poor, they took care to watch out for one another. One of the men was named Kurai. He owned the land on which they lived and worked. The other was called Dau, and he was in charge of the sheep.

One winter, a severe dzhut struck their farm. Soon after, all their sheep starved to death. Dau took Kurai aside and said, "My life has ended. I'll wander into the hills and let the storms take me as well. You've been a fine friend, Kurai. I will miss you."

"No, no, Dau," replied Kurai. "You can't go off and leave me. Who will help with the garden, come spring? Who will tell me stories around the night fire? I want you here, on the land with me. I'm giving you half ownership of the field. You take the lower half, and I'll keep the upper part. The deed is already in your name."

A rare and wonderful thing happened the following spring. Dau was digging in his half of the field and struck something made of metal with his hoe. He dug deeper into the black earth and uncovered a small, iron chest. It was filled with gold coins. He ran to Kurai, shouting, "You are rich! You can live like a kahn. And you deserve it, Kurai, for you are a good man."

Kurai said, "You found the gold in your half of the field, Dau. The treasure is yours, and yours alone. I'm truly happy for you."

"No, my generous friend," explained Dau. "The gold is yours. You have given me my life. How can I take anything more?"

"God has given you the gold," said Kurai.

"How can I take from God that which He has given to you?"

"Enough of your stubbornness!" cried Dau. "Take the gold."

"Enough of your nonsense!" replied Kurai. "The gold is yours."

The two friends argued long into the night. Neither gave in to the other. They were exhausted by morning and decided to talk with a teacher who lived in the middle of the steppes. He was known as the wisest man in the region. It took five days to find the wise man's hut. The two friends showed him the gold and told him of their argument. The teacher looked at the coins and then at the men. He looked again at the coins and again at the men. Then he closed his eyes and thought and thought. After a long while, he opened his eyes and said, "Take the gold to the city and buy the highest quality seeds in the land. Return to your fields and plant the finest orchard in the steppes. Make it an orchard of friendship. Allow the poor to rest in its shade, eat of its fruit, and enjoy its beauty. Rather than divide two friends, let the gold serve many."

Kurai and Dau agreed, and left for the city. They arrived several days later and headed for the marketplace. They searched and searched for a seller of fruit seeds, but had no luck. No one had seeds to sell. The old men were tired and decided to rest for the night and try again the following day. On the way to an inn, they heard a terrible screeching coming from a thousand caged birds, carried by a caravan of camels. The colorful birds had been captured in the thick forests and high mountains, and were being taken to market. They would be sold as food for wealthy tables.

Kurai looked at Dau and said, "It isn't good to be put in a cage." Dau looked at Kurai and said, "It isn't right that beautiful birds should be eaten by the rich." They approached the leader of the caravan and asked the price of the birds. He looked at their poor clothes and said, "More than you have."

Kurai opened the iron chest. "Release them and the gold is yours," he said. Dau nodded his head in agreement. The leader ordered his helpers to set the birds free. Up into the sky they flew, singing songs of joy! Kurai and Dau began their long walk home, feeling happy for the birds, but sad for the orchard that would never be. They talked about their long friendship and decided that it was foolish to argue. Arriving home a few days later, they witnessed a strange sight.

A thousand beautiful birds sat in their field and scratched in the dirt. Each held a seed in its beak and dropped it into the loose soil. The dirt was smoothed over the seeds with the beating of strong wings. Then, creating a multicolored cloud of feather and song, the birds rose into the sky and flew away. Rain fell and the seeds sprouted, climbing slowly from earth toward sky. The orchard took root. Apple trees and pear trees and apricot, too. Trees take time to grow, and the two old men passed on before they could taste the first of the fruit. Kurai and Dau were not saddened, however, as they had eaten from the fruit of friendship for so many years.

※ ※ ※

Dzhut: The lack of food for livestock in winter in regions of nomadic livestock raising. The condition is caused by the formation of ice in pastures, following storms.

Steppe: Vast grasslands, with few trees, except near running water

Khan: A ruler of the Mongols, Tartars, or Turkic/Altaic peoples of Central Asia.

QUESTIONS

§ *Why do you think Dau and Kurai argue over who should keep the gold?*

§ *What do you think of the wise man's advice to the two friends?*

§ *If you hadn't heard the story, what would you think it was about, just from hearing the title?*

SIX

GIVING AND FORGIVING

Without forgiveness, there's no future.

—DESMOND TUTU

We all make mistakes. That's how we learn and grow. Generosity is present when we recognize each other's potential to do good, rather than limiting our perception of the other to one single act that caused harm. Forgiveness makes room for relationships to flourish. Forgiving means foregoing judgment and cultivating compassion. It means honoring the complexity of being human. Stories of making amends can remind us of the many factors that lead people to hurt each other through their speech and through their actions. Stories also offer many points of entry for exploring what it means to take responsibility for our actions and do the best we can to repair the harm we have caused. Wherever people live in community there will be conflict. How that community addresses conflict will make the difference to its health. Removing offenders from the community may be necessary at times, but there are alternatives. One of these is Restorative Justice, a movement that is gaining momentum in Canada and the United States in a number of settings, from communities to schools.[18] In the Restorative Justice circle as it is used in schools, peers facilitate the conversation, in which both offender and those affected by the offender's actions are present, learning about each other and working together to come up with a plan for restitution.

---

18 See Bringing Restorative Justice Into Schools, a program of Tri-county Restorative Justice. http://tricountyrestorativejustice.com/index.html

A Blind Man Catches a Bird

ZIMBABWE

Among the Xhosa and Zulu-speaking people of South Africa, an imbongi is a traditional praise poet, or a praise singer. These are the custodians of oral tradition. They are called "praise poets" because they sometimes exaggerate the qualities of leaders at important public events, but they also use their popularity and status as the voice of the ancestors as a platform for social criticism. This ancient form of verbal art remains a vibrant, highly developed genre in Southern Africa.

A young man married a woman whose brother was blind. The young man was eager to get to know his new brother-in-law and so he asked him if he would like to go hunting with him.

"I cannot see," the blind man said. "But you can help me see when we are out hunting together. We can go."

The young man led the blind man off into the bush. At first they followed a path that he knew and it was easy for him to tag along behind the other. After a while, though, they went off into thicker bush, where the trees grew closely together and there were many places for animals to hide. The blind man now held on to the arm of his sighted brother-in-law and told him many things about the sounds that they heard around them. Because he had no sight, he had a great ability to interpret the noises made by animals in the bush.

"There are warthogs around," he would say. "I can hear their noises over there."

Or, "That bird is preparing to fly. Listen to the sound of its wings unfolding."

To the brother-in-law, these sounds were meaningless, and he was most impressed at the blind man's ability to understand the bush although it must have been for him one great darkness.

They walked on for several hours, until they reached a place where they could set their traps. The blind man followed the other's advice, and put his trap in a place where birds might come for water. The other man put his trap a short distance away, taking care to disguise it so that no bird would know that it was there. He did not bother to disguise the blind man's trap, as it was hot and he was eager to get home to his new wife. The blind man thought that his brother-in-law had disguised his trap, but since he could not see, he didn't know that he failed to do so.

They returned to their hunting place the next day. The blind man was excited at the prospect of having caught something, and the young man had to tell him to keep quiet, or he would scare all the animals away. Even before they reached the traps, the blind man was able to tell that they had caught something.

"I can hear birds," he said. "There are birds in the traps."

When he reached his trap, the young man saw that he had caught a small bird. He took it out of the trap and put it in a pouch that he had brought with him. Then the two of them walked towards the blind man's trap.

"There's a bird in it," the young man said to his blind brother-in-law. "You have caught a bird too."

As he spoke, he felt himself filling with jealousy. The blind man's bird was marvelously coloured, as if it had flown through a rainbow and been stained by colours. The feathers from a bird such as that would make a fine present for his new wife, but the blind man had a wife too, and she would also want the feathers.

The young man bent down and took the bird from the blind man's trap. Then, quickly substituting his own bird, he passed it to the blind man and put the colored bird in his own pouch.

"Here is your bird," the young man said to the blind man. "You may put it in your pouch."

The blind man reached out for the bird and took it. He felt it for a moment, his fingers passing over the wings and the breast. Then, without saying anything, he put the bird into his pouch and they began the trip home.

On their way home, the two men stopped to rest under a broad tree. As they sat there, they talked about many things. The young man was impressed with the wisdom of the blind man, who knew a great deal, although he could see nothing at all.

"Why do people fight with one another?" he asked the blind man. It was a question which had always troubled him and he wondered if the blind man could give him an answer.

The blind man said nothing for a few moments, but it was clear to the young man that he was thinking. Then the blind man raised his head, and it seemed to the young man as if the unseeing eyes were staring right into his soul. Quietly he gave his answer.

"Men fight because they do to each other what you have just done to me."

The words shocked the young man and made him ashamed. He tried to think of a response, but none came. Rising to his feet, he fetched his pouch, took out the brightly coloured bird and gave it back to the blind man.

The blind man took the bird, felt it over with his fingers, and smiled.

"Do you have any other questions for me?" he asked.

"Yes," said the young man. "How do men become friends after they have fought?"

The blind man smiled again.

"They do what you have just done," he said. "That's how they become friends again."

🜲 🜼 🜲

QUESTIONS

§ *Do you have any questions about this story?*

§ *How do you think the blind man knew that the hunter had taken his bird?*

§ *Why didn't he say anything right away?*

§ *Why do you think the hunter asked the blind man why men fight?*

§ *Where is generosity in this story?*

The Lady's Loaf-field

SCOTTISH

With its long history of battles and bloodshed, Scotland is often described as the most haunted country in the world. It is said that for some time after the battle of Culloden Moor, in 1746, the local people could watch a re-enactment of the event, fought by two phantom armies.

The Scots have acquired a reputation for being "careful," (stingy). As with all people, however, learning to give just requires a little practice.

There was once an old laird who loved only two things in the world. They were his wife and his money, and it would have been hard to decide which of the two of them came first with him. He loved his wife enough to give her anything she asked him for—always hoping it wouldn't cost him too much. And he loved his money so much that the only one who could get any of it away from him at all was his wife.

She, poor lady, never asked for much for herself, but she had a great pity for the troubles and sorrows of the poor folks round about. She would ask for them, and although the laird would never give her as much as she asked him for, he always gave her something, which helped somewhat.

Well, the good lady, who had never been strong, fell into an illness, and although the laird and everyone else thought she'd soon be well again, she knew better. So she began to fret to herself about her poor folks and wonder what in the world they'd do when she wasn't there to look after them.

At last she asked the laird to set aside a field to grow grain in, to make loaves for the poor, which they might have for the asking. Well, at first the laird wouldn't hear to it at all. But when she told him it was likely to be the last thing she'd ever be asking him in this life, he grew a little bit frightened. He didn't believe her at all, but to set her mind at ease, he told her that she might have any field of his that she could walk around. He thought she'd have to wait until she was well again to do the walking and by that time maybe she'd have forgotten all about it.

But the lady was too clever for him entirely. The next day she called to her two strong lasses that worked in the castle, and had them take her into the fields. There, she picked out one of the best of the laird's grain fields and then she laid her arms across the lasses' shoulders and, with them supporting her on either side, she walked all the way around the field.

When she went back and told the laird what she'd done, he was put out about it, but he had to admit the field was hers, for she'd walked around it and the two lasses could prove it.

The lady was right about it being the last thing she'd ask of him. Not long afterward she died. When she was dying, she told him not to be forgetting about the field he'd given her for her poor folks, and never to be taking it back for himself; because if he did, she'd be sure to know about it.

Well, the old laird set the field aside as he had promised, and he had it plowed and harrowed and seeded year by year. And, year by year, the grain grew better on that field than it did on any of the others. He had the grain reaped and threshed and winnowed and ground, and it was all kept to make loaves for the poor folks. So none of the poor folks round about ever went hungry, because when they wanted a loaf of bread all they needed to do was to ask at the castle of one of the lady's loaves.

The years went by, and now that his lady was gone, the laird had nothing to love but his money, so he began to love that twice as much as he'd ever done before. And he began to cast his eye on the lady's loaf-field, and figure out so many loaves at so many pennies a loaf for so many years past and to come. The amount of money he was losing through that foolish promise was beyond bearing. To make his conscience easy, he told himself that she hadn't really walked around the field herself at all, for she'd had the help of a strapping young lass on either side of her. So he wouldn't be breaking a promise if he took the field for himself after all.

When plowing time came next year, he made up his mind that this time the grain that was grown was going to make money for his pocket and not loaves for the poor.

The word soon got around that there'd be no more loaves at the castle, after the present supply was gone. When the poor folks heard that they couldn't believe their ears. The sound of their grief rose on the air and grew until it reached heaven.

But the laird was set on having his way. The field was plowed and harrowed and seeded, and the grain grew and was reaped and taken to the barn to be threshed and winnowed. But it was not kept to itself to be threshed and gathered into sacks to be ground for the poor folks' loaves. Instead, the laird gave orders that the whole of it was to be thrown in with his own, for he was going to sell it all, and there was to be no more foolishness about the lady's loaf-field.

The next day after that was the one set for the threshing. The men who were to do it were up before daybreak, because there was such a grand heap of grain to be threshed and it being harvest time there was no time to spare. Three or four of them, that were ready first, went to the barn to get the threshing floor and the flails ready for the rest of the men who'd soon be coming along.

They went into the barn laughing and talking, for harvest time is a merry time, what with the jokes and games and feasting that come at the end. But they came out shrieking, and faster than they went in. They rushed along to the castle and met the laird coming out of it on his way up to the barn. They all tried to tell him at the same time, but what with the fright they had on them and the way their teeth chattered and losing their breath running so fast, all that he could make out of what they were trying to say was that there was a ghost and it was in the barn.

"A ghost," said the laird with disgust. "You're a pack o' fools! More like 'tis naught but the old white mare."

So he stomped off up to the barn and in he went.

And there was a ghost there. It sat upon the top of one of the heaps of grain, and it was the ghost of his own dead lady.

When she saw him she rose up and she pointed a ghostly finger at him.

"I walked the field on my own two feet," said she, "and you gave it me for my own. If you do not thresh my grain for my poor folks' loaves, there'll never be grain threshed in this barn again, for I'll sit here till the end of time ere I e'er let a flail touch a sheaf on this barn's floor."

Well, the laird knew when he was beaten. So he promised the good lady's ghost that he'd never think of breaking his promise again. When she was sure he meant it, she up and disappeared.

The laird had a very difficult time getting the men to come back, but at last he did. The laird had had such a bad fright, he wanted to make sure that there'd be no further trouble. Since he had no way now to tell which were his lady's sheaves and which were his own, having had them all dumped together the way they were, he told the men to thresh all the grain and put it into sacks to be ground. And all of the grain grown on the castle fields that year was made into loaves for the poor folks roundabout. That was a wonderful year for the poor folks, because when one of them was hungry and went to the castle to ask for a loaf of bread, he was given not one but two. And the sound of the poor folks rejoicing grew and increased until it reached heaven. The laird's lady heard it there and was content. She knew the old laird had learned his lesson

Indeed he had, for he left it in his will that his heirs should always keep that field for the poor. It is so kept until this very day. If you should ever be traveling in those parts you can go up to the castle, and if you just step in and ask they'll take you out and show you the lady's loaf-field.

❦ ❦ ❦

Laird: Lord of the manor or lord of the castle

Lass: Young woman

Strapping: Strong

Flail: A tool made of a long wooden handle or staff and a shorter, free-swinging stick attached to its end

Thresh: To beat the stems and husks of grain or cereal plants with a machine or flail, to separate the grains or seeds from the straw.

Sheaf: A bundle of cut stalks of grain or similar plants bound with straw or twine

Chaff: Thin dry scales that cover or enclose grains of wheat and some other cereal grasses. These are removed during threshing.

Winnow: To separate the chaff from the grain by means of a current of air.

Harrow: (*noun*) A tool, usually formed of pieces of timber or metal crossing each other, and set with iron or wooden teeth. It is drawn over plowed land to level it and break the clods, to stir the soil and make it fine, or to cover seed when sown.

Harrow: (*verb*) To draw a harrow over the field for the purpose of breaking clods or clumps of earth and leveling the surface, or for covering seed; as, to harrow land.

Plough/plow: The plough or plow is a tool used in farming for initial cultivation of soil in preparation for sowing seed or planting. The primary purpose of ploughing is to turn over the upper layer of the soil, bringing fresh nutrients to the surface, while burying weeds and the remains of previous crops, allowing them to break down.

Threshing-floor: Floor of the barn where the threshing took place.

QUESTIONS

What different kinds of giving are present in this story?

Have you ever made a promise that was difficult to keep? What happened?

How did the Lady make sure the Laird kept his promise?

What kinds of gifts can we leave to future generations? How?

The Clever Sheik of the Butana

SUDAN

*In Sudan, storytelling is the province of the older
women in the village, and tales were often told as
children gathered around to eat sorghum or mil-
let porridge from one large pot. As the children
listen with wide eyes, the storyteller draws out the
syllables to emphasize distance, danger, or size—
kabiiir for 'big', and baiiiiid for 'far'. Each telling of
the story will be different, with audience members
participating, and the storyteller adapting the story
for a particular occasion.*

Many tents were scattered over a wide range of the Butana, that piece of
land that lies east of the river known as the Blue Nile in the Sudan. The
tents marked the capital of Sheik Hamad, who was the ruler of the tribes
that lived in the Butana.

One day Sheik Hamad received a visitor, who was on his way to a far-off town. The
traveler was hosted very generously by Sheikh Hamad, as is the custom of the Sudanese.
The Sheikh slew a big ox for the visitor and asked all the people to come for supper with
the traveler. They had their supper and after that they sat listening to songs of bravery
and stories of how they defeated their opponents from different tribes. They listened to
music played on a flute called a *zumbara*, and every tune, or *loda*, told of a certain event.

At last, in the middle of the night, the feast came to an end and the guest was
taken to his tent to sleep.

In the morning, unfortunately, the guest found that his money was gone, all of
it. It had been stolen. A thief had broken into the tent while the people of the tribe
were honoring the guest and making the feast for him.

The guest told Sheik Hamad about the theft. Sheik Hamad said to him, "Don't
tell anybody about this. In the evening, when all the people come to the feast, we
shall get your money back."

The day passed very slowly, and the guest spent the long hours thinking about his lost money, if it was going to be returned to him, and how.

In the evening, another ox was slain for the guest and the people of the tribe. The Sheik's four wives, the women of the tribe, and the servants cooked the food. All the people were invited and all of them came.

After they had eaten, enjoyed themselves, listened to many songs and *zumbara lodas*, Sheikh Hamad stood up and addressed the people. "Well, our guest has lost all his money. Whoever took it or found it lying on the ground, let him step forward now and give it back." Nobody came forward.

Then the Sheikh said to them, "My donkey is in that tent. I want every man here to enter the tent, take hold of the donkey's tail, then come out the other entrance. Make sure you hold the tail of the donkey. If the one who holds the tail is innocent, nothing will happen to him, but when the one who has taken the money holds the tail, the donkey will bray. So go."

The first man entered and came out by the other door. Nothing happened. The second did the same. Nothing happened. The third, the fourth. But still nothing happened. Every man entered and came out, but the donkey didn't make any sound.

The Sheikh then asked the men to stand in a row and he went from one to the next. He took each man's hands, put them near his face, and then let them go. One by one he did this. Then the Sheikh took the hands of one of the men, put them near his face, very near his nose, and ordered him to step out.

He said to the man, "You have stolen the money. I want it brought now." The man tried his best to deny it, but Sheikh Hamad told him that the more he denied it, the worse his punishment would be. The Sheikh whispered in the thief's ear, "I oiled the donkey's tail with scented *dihn* oil. All the innocent people took hold of it and the scent of the *dihn* was in their palms, but, because you were afraid that the donkey might bray, you didn't hold it. And the *dihn* scent didn't get on your hands. Bring the money now, or you will curse the day on which your mother gave birth to you."

The man, accompanied by two of the Sheikh's guards went away, dug a hole in ground, and brought the money. The man promised not to do such a thing ever again. He was forgiven and was given part of the money to start a new, honest life.

⚘ ⚘ ⚘

QUESTIONS

§ *What customs of hospitality do you know?*

§ *How does the Sheik trick the thief into revealing himself?*

§ *Was the thief given any punishment?*

Strawberries

CHEROKEE

The Cherokee word for strawberry is ani. The rich bottomlands of the old Cherokee country were noted for their abundance of strawberries and other wild fruits. Before there were humans on this earth, there was no argument. There was no quarrelling and therefore, no need for forgiveness. But now that we are here, we human beings get angry; we hold grudges; we bicker and quarrel and refuse to make up. Even today, strawberries are often kept in Cherokee homes. They remind us not to argue and are a symbol of good luck.

Long ago, in the very first days of the world, there lived the first man and the first woman. They lived together as husband and wife, and they loved one another dearly.

But there came a day when that first man and that first woman had their first quarrel. Later, neither could remember what the quarrel was about, but harsh and ugly words were spoken and pain flew back and forth between them, until finally, in anger and in grief, the woman left their home and began walking away. She was walking east, toward the rising sun.

The man sat alone in his house. But as time went by, he grew lonelier and lonelier. The anger left him and all that remained was a terrible grief and despair, and he began to cry.

Creator, the provider of all good things, heard the man crying and took pity on him, saying, "Man, why do you cry?"

The man said, "My wife has left me."

"Why did your woman leave?" asked Creator.

The man just hung his head and said nothing.

"You quarreled with her," said Creator.

And the man nodded.

"Tell me this," said Creator, "if your wife were to return, would you quarrel with her again?"

The man said, "No." He wanted only to live with his wife as they had lived before, in peace, in happiness, and in love.

"Well then I will tell you, I have seen your woman," Creator said. "She is walking to the east toward the rising sun."

The man began following his wife, but he could not overtake her. Everyone knows an angry woman walks fast!

Finally, Creator said, "I'll go ahead and see if I can make her slow her steps." So Creator went on ahead and found the woman walking, her footsteps fast and angry and her gaze fixed straight ahead. There was pain and anger still in her heart.

Creator saw some huckleberry bushes growing along the trail, so with a wave of his hand, he made the bushes burst into bloom and ripen into fruit. But the woman's gaze remained fixed. She looked neither to the right nor the left, and she didn't see the berries. Her footsteps did not slow.

Then Creator saw some blueberry bushes growing along the trail. Again, Creator waved his hand, and one by one, all of the berries growing along the trail burst into bloom and ripened into fruit. But still, the woman saw nothing but her anger, and her footsteps did not slow.

Finally, Creator thought, "I will create an entirely new fruit; one that grows very close to the ground because only by bending her head for a moment will the woman forget her anger." So Creator made a thick green carpet begin to grow along the trail. Then the carpet became starred with tiny white flowers, and each flower gradually ripened into a berry that was the color and shape of the human heart.

As the woman walked, she crushed the tiny berries under her feet, and a delicious smell rose. She stopped, looked down, and saw the berries. She picked one and ate it, and it was as sweet as love itself. So she began walking slowly, picking berries as she went, and as she leaned down to pick a berry, she saw her husband coming behind her.

The anger had gone from her heart, and all that remained was the love she had always known. She stopped and waited for him, and together, they picked and ate the berries. Finally, they returned to their home where they lived out their days in peace, happiness, and love.

And that's how Creator brought the first strawberries into the world. They are the color and shape of the human heart and they were put here to restore peace and love to quarreling men and women.

※ ❦ ※

֍ *Why do you think the first man and the first woman quarreled?*

֍ *How does the passage of time make a difference to both husband and wife?*

SEVEN

SHARING WISDOM

Wisdom is easy to carry but difficult to gather.

—CZECH PROVERB

The stories in this chapter explore the generosity that is present when we share our knowledge and our wisdom. As we know, new learning is reinforced when we put it into practice right away. And when we share it with someone else, our understanding deepens as we recognize how people absorb new ideas and skills each in his or her own way. Telling a story is like this, since everyone will hear something slightly different in it. To find out how children have received a story I will sometimes delay telling them what the title is. Then, when I am finished the story, I ask them for their ideas. I am always curious to hear what element of the story they will choose to highlight. Will it be one of the characters, the principal action, an important object, or something else?

Sharing wisdom isn't just about passing along knowledge. It's also about sharing perspectives, including the way we might inquire into a situation. Often when I have told a story I will ask the children to think about it and write down a question they have. If there is time, we read aloud our questions and propose possible answers. Their queries range from a desire for more factual information, as in "What kind of bird did the blind man catch?" to speculation on a character's abilities—"How did the blind man know the hunter had switched the birds?"— or motives—"Why was the lizard so mean?" This kind of discussion is not about filling in the gaps in the narrative; it's about learning that there are many ways to think about a story.

Stories themselves are bundles of wisdom, ready to be unpacked and put to use wherever they travel. In the literary tale, "The Burning of the Rice Fields," the village headman's memory of a story is what allows him to save the lives of the villagers. When he sees the sea receding from the shoreline he scans his memory for clues to explain this odd occurrence. He quickly realizes that this phenomenon doesn't correspond to anything in his own experience, except for one thing—an image from a story his grandfather told him as a child, saying, "It was as if the sea was running away from the land." From his recollection of the next scene in that story, he knows he has to act quickly to make sure the villagers come away from the shoreline, before the sea returns in the form of a *tsunami*. Knowing a story can save your life.

Hearing stories nurtures flexible thinking, especially when we reflect on them in the company of others. The more we hear a set of stories and the more we tell them, the more meaning they gather. Different contexts and different listeners can shift the emphasis in the story and reveal new layers of significance. Stories enrich our imagination *and* they provide us with tools for understanding the complexity of the world.

Every family has its own store of wisdom, linked to family history, favorite children's books, old songs, proverbs, and rhymes. Ask the children in your class to collect sayings and proverbs from their own families and cultures. Create a class list. This is a beautiful way to celebrate the multi-cultural richness of many classrooms. Read the list out loud every time one is added. Ask the child who collected it to explain how he understands the teaching in the proverb or saying. Notice what common themes run through the phrases. Are there any about giving and receiving?

Why Wisdom is Found Everywhere

GHANA

Tales of the trickster spider Anansi are well known in West Africa. They are now part of North American folklore as well, having crossed the Atlantic to the Caribbean with captives during the Atlantic slave trade. In the Caribbean, Anansi is often celebrated as a symbol of slave resistance and survival.

A long time ago, Anansi the spider had all the wisdom in the world stored in a huge pot. Nyame, the sky god, had given it to him. Anansi had been instructed to share it with everyone. Every day, Anansi looked in the pot, and learned different things. The pot was full of wonderful ideas and skills.

Anansi greedily thought, "I will not share the treasure of knowledge with everyone. I will keep all the wisdom for myself."

So, Anansi decided to hide the wisdom on top of a tall tree. He took some vines and made some strong string and tied it firmly around the pot, leaving one end free. He tied the loose end around his waist so that the pot hung in front of him. Then he started to climb the tree. He struggled as he climbed because the pot of wisdom kept getting in his way, bumping against his belly.

Anansi's son watched in fascination as his father struggled up the tree. Finally, Anansi's son told him "If you tie the pot to your back, it will be easier to cling to the tree and climb."

Anansi tied the pot to his back instead, and continued to climb the tree, with much more ease than before. When Anansi got to the top of the tree, he became angry.

"A young one with some common sense knows more than I, and I have the pot of wisdom!"

In anger, Anansi threw down the pot of wisdom. The pot broke, and pieces of wisdom flew in every direction. People found the bits scattered everywhere, and if they wanted to, they could take some home to their families and friends.

That is why to this day, no one person has *all* the world's wisdom. People everywhere share small pieces of it whenever they exchange ideas.

QUESTIONS

S   *What kind of things might Anansi have learned when he looked into the pot?*

S   *Why does Anansi get so mad when his son gives him advice about how to carry the pot?*

S   *What is common sense?*

S   *Is there a difference between knowledge and wisdom? How would you explain the difference?*

S   *Where does wisdom come from?*

S   *What are some ways we can share wisdom and knowledge?*

The Wise Quail

INDIA

The Wise Quail is one of the Jataka tales—stories told of the Buddha's lives before he was born as a prince. In the Buddhist countries of south-east Asia, these stories are still very much a part of daily life. On the lunar observance days (religious holidays) villagers come to the local temple to hear monks recite the Jataka all night long.

Once, the Buddha was a wise quail, the leader of a flock. One day, a hunter came into the forest. Imitating the quails' own calls, he began to trap unwary birds. The wise quail noticed that something was amiss. Calling his flock together, he announced, "My fellow quail, I am afraid that there is a hunter in our forest. Many of our brothers and sisters are missing. We must be alert. Danger is all around us. Still, if we work together we can stay free. Please listen to my plan. If you should hear a whistling call—twe whee! twe whee! twe whee!—as if a brother or sister were calling, be very watchful! If you follow that call, you may find darkness descending upon you. Your wings may be pinned so that you cannot fly, and the fear of death may grip your heart. If these things happen, just understand that you have been trapped by the hunter's net and do not give up! Remember, if you work together you can be free.

"Now, this is my plan. You must stick your heads out through the webs of the net and, then, you must all flap your wings together. As a group, though you are still bound in the net, you will rise up into the air. Fly to a bush. Let the net drape on the branches of the bush so you can each drop to the ground, and fly away from under the net, this way and that, to freedom. Do you understand? Can you do this?"

"We do understand," answered all the quail as one, "and we will do it! We will work together and be free."

Hearing this, the wise quail was content. The very next day a group of quail were pecking on the ground when they heard a long whistling call. "Twe whee! twe whee! twe whee!" It was the cry of a quail in distress! Off they rushed. Suddenly darkness descended on them and their wings were pinned. They had indeed been trapped by the hunter's net. But, remembering the wise quail's words, they did not panic. Sticking their heads out through the webs of the net they flapped their wings together, harder and harder, and slowly, slowly, with the net still draped upon them, they rose, as a group, through the air. They flew to a bush. They dropped down through the bush, leaving the net hung on the outer branches, then flew away, each in their own direction, this way and that, to freedom.

The plan had worked! They were safe! They had escaped from the jaws of death. And, oh, they were happy!

But the hunter was not happy. He could not understand how the quail had escaped him. And this happened not just once, but many times. At last, the hunter realized the truth. "Why," he said, amazed, "those quail are cooperating! They are working together! But it can't last. They are only birds, featherbrains after all. Sooner or later they will argue. And when they do, I shall have them." And so, he was patient.

Now, the wise quail had had the same thought. Sooner or later the birds of his flock would begin to argue, and when that happened they would be lost. So he decided to take them deeper into the forest, far from their present danger.

That very day something happened to confirm the wise quail's thought. A quail was pecking on the ground for seeds when another bird of the flock, descending rapidly, accidentally struck it with its wing-tip. "Hey! Watch it, stupid!" called the first quail, in anger.

"Stupid is it?" responded the newly-landed quail, flustered because he had been careless. "Why are you so high and mighty? You were too dumb to move out of my way! Yes, you were too dumb, you dumb cluck!"

"Dumb cluck is it?" cried the first quail, "Dumb cluck? Why, talking of dumb, it's clear that you can't even land without slapping someone in the face! If that isn't 'dumb,' I don't know what is! Who taught you to fly anyway—the naked-winged bats?"

"Bats is it?" yelled the second quail, enraged, "Bats? Why, I'll give you a bat, you feathered ninny!" And with a loud chirruping whistle he hurled himself straight at the other quail. Chasing furiously after one another, loudly hurling insults and threats back and forth, they flew, twisting and turning, between the great, silent trees of the grove. An argument had started and, as is the way of arguments, no end was in sight.

The wise quail was nearby and he heard it all. At once he knew that danger was again upon them. If they could not work together the hunter was sure to have them. So again he called his flock together and said, "My dear brother and sister quail. The hunter is here. Let us go elsewhere, deeper into the forest and there, in seclusion, discipline ourselves, practicing our skills in working together. In this way we shall become truly free from the danger."

Many of the birds said, "Though we love our present home, we shall go with you, Wise Quail. The danger is great and we wish to find safety."

But others said, "Why go from this pleasant spot? You yourself, Wise Quail, have taught us all we need to know in order to be free. We know what to do. We just have to stick our heads out, flap our wings together, and fly away. Any dumb cluck can do it! We're going to stay."

So some of the birds flew off with the wise quail, while the others stayed. A few days later, while some of those who stayed were scratching around for their dinner, they heard a whistling call. "Twe whee! twe whee! twe whee!" They ran to answer the call when suddenly, darkness descended upon them. Fear gripped their hearts. They were trapped in the hunter's net! But, remembering the wise quail's teaching, they stuck their heads through the net, and one bird said, "On the count of three we all flap. Ready? One two, three . . . "

"Hey!" called another bird, "Who made you boss? Who said you could give the orders?"

"I'm the hardest worker and the strongest," said the first bird. "When I flap my wings, the dust rises from the earth and whirls up in clouds. Without me you'd never get this net off the ground. So I give the orders, see?"

"No, I don't see!" shouted another bird. "What you've just described is nothing. Why, when I flap my wings, all the leaves move on the trees, the branches bend and even the trunks sway. That's how strong I am. So if anyone should be giving orders around here it's me!"

"No, me!" shouted a third bird.

"Me!" yelled a fourth.

"No! No! Listen to me!" screamed the first bird again above the rising din. "Flap Flap! Flap! I tell you. Flap your wings all together when I say 'three!'"

But no one flapped. They just argued and argued. And as they argued, the hunter came along and found them and their fate, alas, was not a happy one. But the quail who had gone off deeper into the safety of the great forest learned, under the wise quail's guidance, how to really cooperate. They practiced constantly, until they were, indeed, able to work together without anger or argument. Though the hunter tried many times to catch them he never could. And if he never caught them, why, they're still free today.

❧ *What is cooperation? Can you give examples?*

❧ *Why does it take practice to work together successfully?*

❧ *How might the quail have practiced? How and when do you practice at home or at school?*

❧ *What is the hardest part of cooperation or collaboration?*

❧ *What is the most rewarding?*

The Burning of the Rice Fields

JAPAN

This story comes from the writings of Lafcadio Hearn, an American who lived in Japan in the late 19th century. Hearn was in Tokyo in 1896, when a wave two hundred miles long struck the north-eastern provinces of Miyagi, Iwaté, and Aomori. At that time he heard of a tsunami which struck the coast of Japan more than a century earlier. Hearn begins his story by describing the communal obligation of every villager, young and old, to help each other in a time of danger such as a fire or flood.

Hamaguchi Gohei was the headman of the village to which he belonged. The villagers held him in high regard. They were also very fond of him. They called him *Ojiisan*, which means Grandfather. Hamaguchi was also the richest member of the community. He had many fields in rice production. He advised the smaller farmers and loaned them money. He helped them resolve their disputes and dispose of their rice on the best terms possible.

Hamaguchei's big thatched farmhouse stood at the verge of a small plateau overlooking a bay. The plateau, mostly devoted to rice culture, was hemmed in on three sides by thick woods. The verge of the plateau sloped down in a huge green basin, as if scooped out, to the edge of the water. The whole of this slope was terraced and resembled an enormous flight of green steps, divided in the centre by a narrow white zigzag—a streak of mountain road.

The village was made up of ninety thatched dwellings and a Shintô temple which stood along the curve of the bay. Other houses climbed straggling up the slope for some distance on either side of the narrow road leading to Hamaguchi's home.

One autumn evening Hamaguchi was sitting on the balcony of his house, watching the activities in the village below. There had been a fine rice-crop, and the peasants were going to celebrate their harvest by a dance. The old man could see the festival banners (the *nobori*) fluttering above the roofs of the solitary street, the strings of paper lanterns festooned between bamboo poles, the decorations of the shrine, and the brightly colored gathering of the young people. He had nobody with him that evening but his little grandson, a boy of ten; the rest of the household having gone early to the village. He would have accompanied them had he not been feeling less strong than usual. The day had been oppressive; and in spite of a rising breeze there was still in the air that sort of heavy heat which, according to the experience of the Japanese peasant, at certain seasons precedes an earthquake.

And presently an earthquake came.

It was not strong enough to frighten anybody; but Hamaguchi, who had felt hundreds of shocks in his time, thought it was queer—a long, slow, spongy motion. Probably it was but the after-tremor of some immense seismic action very far away. The house crackled and rocked gently several times; then all became still again.

Hamaguchi turned his keen old eyes toward the village. He rose to his feet, and looked at the sea. It had darkened and was acting strangely. It seemed to be moving against the wind.

The sea was running away from the land.

As the sea receded, things never seen before became visible; spaces of ribbed sand and reaches of weed-hung rock were left bare. And none of the people below who were now gathering at the shore appeared to guess what that monstrous ebb signified. Hamaguchi himself had never seen such a thing before; but as he gazed, he remembered this very image from a story told to him in his childhood by his grandfather.

He remembered his grandfather saying, "Yes, it was as if the sea had chosen to run away from the land."

But what happened next in the story? Where did the sea go? Hamaguchi searched his memory. And then he remembered.

He called to his grandson: "Tada! Quick . . . Light me a torch."

Taimatsu, or pine-torches, are kept in many coast dwellings for use on stormy nights. The child kindled a torch at once; and the old man hurried with it to the fields, where hundreds of rice-stacks, stood drying in the autumn sunshine. He began to set the torch to those nearest the verge of the slope—hurrying from one to another as quickly as his aged limbs could carry him. The sun-dried stalks caught like tinder; the strengthening sea breeze blew the blaze landward; the stacks burst into flame, sending skyward columns of smoke that met and mingled into one enormous cloudy whirl.

Tada, astonished and terrified, ran after his grandfather, crying, "Ojiisan! Why? Ojiisan! Why? Why?"

But Hamaguchi did not answer. He had no time to explain. He was thinking only of the four hundred villagers in danger.

For a while the child stared wildly at the blazing rice; then burst into tears, and ran back to the house, feeling sure that his grandfather had gone mad.

Hamaguchi went on, firing stack after stack, till he had reached the limit of his field; then he threw down his torch, and waited. The acolyte of the hill-temple, observing the blaze, set the big bell booming; and the people responded to the double appeal. Hamaguchi watched them hurrying in from the sands and over the beach and up from the village, like a swarming of ants, and, to his anxious eyes, scarcely faster; for the moments seemed terribly long to him.

The sun was going down; the wrinkled bed of the bay, and a vast sallow speckled expanse beyond it, lay naked to the last orange glow; and still the sea was fleeing toward the horizon.

Really, however, Hamaguchi did not have very long to wait before the first party arrived—a score of agile young peasants, who wanted to attack the fire at once.

But Hamaguchi, holding out both arms, stopped them.

"Let it burn, lads!" he commanded, "let it be! I want the whole *mura* here. There is a great danger."

The whole village was coming; and Hamaguchi counted.

All the young men and boys were soon on the spot, and not a few of the more active women and girls; then came most of the older folk, and mothers with babies at their backs, and even children, for children could help to pass water; and the elders too feeble to keep up with the first rush could be seen well on their way up the steep ascent. The growing multitude, still knowing nothing, looked alternately, in sorrowful wonder, at the flaming fields and at the impassive face of their Ojiisan.

And the sun went down.

"Grandfather is mad,—I am afraid of him!" sobbed Tada, in answer to a number of questions. "He is mad. He set fire to the rice on purpose: I saw him do it!"

"As for the rice," cried Hamaguchi, "the child tells the truth. I set fire to the rice. . . . Are all the people here?"

The heads of families looked about them, and down the hill, and made reply:

"All are here, or very soon will be . . . We cannot understand this thing."

"*Kita!*" shouted the old man pointing.

Through the twilight eastward all turned and looked. At the edge of the horizon they saw a long, lean, dim line like the shadowing of a coast where no coast ever was, a line that thickened as they gazed, that broadened as a coast-line broadens to the eyes of one approaching it, yet incomparably more quickly. For that long darkness was the returning sea, towering like a cliff, and approaching more swiftly than the kite flies.

"*Tsunami!*" shrieked the people; and then all shrieks and all sounds and all power to hear sounds were annihilated by a nameless shock heavier than any thunder, as the colossal swell struck the shore with a weight that sent a shudder through the hills, and with a foam-burst like a blaze of sheet-lightning. Then for an instant nothing was visible but a storm of spray rushing up the slope like a cloud; and the people scattered back in panic. They saw the sea washing over the place of their homes. It drew back roaring, and tearing out the bowels of the land as it went. Twice, thrice, five times the sea struck and ebbed, but each time with lesser surges: then it returned to its ancient bed and stayed, still raging, as after a typhoon.

On the plateau for a time there was no word spoken. All stared speechlessly at the desolation beneath. The village was no longer there. Most of the fields were gone. There remained nothing of any of the houses except two straw roofs tossing in the turbulent waves. The after-terror of the death escaped and the bewilderment of the general loss kept everyone speechless, until the voice of Hamaguchi was heard again, observing gently, "That was why I set fire to the rice."

He, their headman, now stood among them almost as poor as the poorest; for his wealth was gone—but he had saved four hundred lives by the sacrifice. His grandson ran to him, and caught his hand, and asked forgiveness for having said he was mad. Whereupon the people realized why they were alive. They began to wonder at the simple, unselfish foresight that had saved them; and they bowed in the dust before Hamaguchi Gohei.

Then the old man wept a little, partly because he was happy, and partly because he was aged and weak and had been sorely tried.

"My house remains," he said, as soon as he could find words; "and there is room for many. Also the temple on the hill stands; and there is shelter there for the others."

Then he led the way to his house; and the people cried and shouted.

The period of distress was long, because in those days there were no means of quick communication between district and district, and the help needed had to be sent from far away. But when better times came, the people did not forget their debt to Hamaguchi Gohei. They built a temple in his honour. A hundred years and more he has been dead; but his temple, they tell me, still stands, and the people still pray to the ghost of the good old farmer to help them in time of fear or trouble.

※ ❧ ※

Ojiisan: Affectionate term for grandfather.

Nobori: Festival banners. A particular kind of *nobori* are the *koinobori* or "carp-streamers." Made by drawing carp patterns on paper or cloth, these windsocks are traditionally flown in Japan to celebrate a national holiday, Kodomo no Hi, or Children's Day which happens early in May.

Taimatsu: Pine torches

Acolyte: Temple attendant

Shinto temple: *Shintoism* is the indigenous spirituality of Japan. Shinto is involved in every aspect of Japanese culture: It touches ethics, politics, family life and social structures, artistic life (particularly drama and poetry) and sporting life (Sumo wrestling), as well as spiritual life. Many events that would be secular in the West involve a brief Shinto ritual in Japan—for example, the construction of a new building would involve a Shinto ceremony.

QUESTIONS

ॐ *Why did Hamaguchi Gohei set fire to his rice harvest?*

ॐ *How was the story he remembered hearing from his grandfather important?*

All Things are Connected

ZAIRE

Traditional storytellers among the Chokwe tribe of Zaire compose their stories while they are telling them. As the listeners respond to the unfolding narrative, the storytellers adapt the tale with the particular audience and situation in mind, referring to current issues and events in the village that are easily identified by the listeners.

Long ago, a cruel chieftain ruled a remote village in Africa. He was a tyrant who demanded that his orders be obeyed on pain of death. Everyone lived in fear of him but for an elderly grandmother who had lived long and seen much. She was the only person in the village brave enough to tell the chief the truth.

The village was located near a large marsh inhabited by numerous amphibians and insects. The people were sung to sleep each night by the gentle croaking of frogs. "Crribbitt, crribbitt, crribbitt."

One night the chief awoke from a bad dream, and couldn't get back to sleep. "Crribbitt, crribbitt, crribbitt" was all he heard. Because he was in a foul mood, the frog's song wasn't at all soothing. It was most irritating. "Crribbitt, crribbitt, crribbitt."

"Quiet!" cried the chief. "I want all the frogs to stop croaking! I demand silence, and I want it now!"

The frogs weren't used to taking orders from humans, and kept on singing. "Crribbitt, crribbitt, crribbitt."

The frogs kept him awake for the rest of the night, and the chief wanted revenge. He called the people together early the next morning, and said, "The frogs disobeyed me. Go to the marsh with your sticks and kill them. If I hear the croak of a single frog tonight, I'll turn my revenge upon you."

All the villagers, except for the old grandmother, grabbed their sticks and ran to the marsh. "Since you are so old and slow, I'll allow you to stay in the village," said the chief.

"And since you are so foolish in your demands, I'll tell you what is true," said the grandmother. "All things are connected."

"What does that mean?" asked the chief.

"You will see," replied the brave woman. "You will soon see."

A strange silence engulfed the village that night. Without the song of the frogs to lull them to sleep, the villagers were restless. The chief, however, slept soundly, and was convinced that he had made the right decision. Several days later, another sound was heard in the village. Zzzz, zzzz, zzzz. Mosquitoes came in swarms and bit everyone in their sleep. Zzzz, zzzz, zzzz.

The chief awoke in anger, batting a thousand mosquitoes away from his head.

"Leave me alone!" he cried. "Get out of my house or I'll have you killed, too!" The mosquitoes answered by buzzing even louder, and biting him again and again. ZZZZ, ZZZZ, ZZZZ.

The following morning, the chief told his people to return to the marsh and kill all the mosquitoes. It was an impossible task, however, as there were far too many insects. Without frogs to eat the larvae, the mosquito population rapidly increased. Thousands upon thousands were hatched each day, and now they ruled the marsh and everything nearby. The village swarmed with hungry mosquitoes, and the animals, as well as the people, suffered. The villagers secretly packed up their belongings and moved far away during the night.

Now, the chief had no one to rule over. At last he understood what the old grandmother had meant. All things are connected. Crribbitt, crribbitt, crribbitt . . .

§ *Why do you think the old grandmother was brave enough to speak boldly to the chief?*

§ *What do you think she meant when she said, "All things are connected?"*

§ *What things are you connected to?*

Notes on the Stories

Page 35 "A Drum" in *Folktales from India: A Selection of Oral Tales from Twenty-two Languages* by A. K. Ramanujan (New York: Pantheon Books, 1991).

Page 39 "An Ox for a Persimmon" in *Korean Folk and Fairy Tales,* retold by Suzanne Crowder Ham and published by Hollym Corporation Publishers, New Jersey, 1991.

Page 41 "The Christmas Doll" is an original story by Phyllis Soles of Texada Island, BC. It was recorded by Margo McLoughlin. Notes about the White Service tradition come from Reverend Murray Speer in his blog-post, "The Origin of White Gift Sunday." Claresholm United Church, a Congregation of the United Church of Canada. December 11, 2011. www.claresholmuc.com/2011/12/origin-of-white-gift-sunday.html

Page 44 "The Chief of the Well" is retold by Margo McLoughlin from Harold Courlander, *The Piece of Fire and Other Haitian Tales* (New York: Harcourt, Brace and Jovanovich, Inc., 1964).

Page 47 "Buffalo Into Rooster" is retold by Margo McLoughlin from Indumati Sheorey, *Folktales of Maharashtra* (New Delhi: Sterling Publishers, 1973), p. 63 – 67.

Page 55 "The Antelope, the Woodpecker, and the Turtle" is translated and retold from the Pali by Margo McLoughlin. Pali source: "Kurunga-miga Jataka," in *The Jataka, Vol. 1, Together with Its Commentary, Being the Tales of the Anterior Births of Gotama Buddha, for the first time edited in the original Pali by V . Fausboll* (London: Kegan Paul Trench Trubner & Co., Ltd, 1891).

Page 59 "The Bird That Was Ashamed of Its Feet" is a traditional Cherokee story retold by storyteller Gayle Ross and published in *A Treasury of North American Folktales.* Compiled and annotated by Catherine Peck. (New York: Norton, 1999).

Page 62 "The King of the Animals" is retold by Margo McLoughlin from Harold Courlander, *The Piece of Fire and Other Haitian Tales* (New York: Harcourt, Brace and Jovanovich, Inc., 1964).

Page 65 "The Value of Salt" in *Korean Folk and Fairy Tales.* Retold by Suzanne Crowder Han. (Hollyn, 1991).

Page 68 "The Friendship Orchard" in *Eleven Nature Tales: A Multicultural Journey* by Pleasant DeSpain. (Little Rock, Arkansas: August House Publishers, 1996).

Page 72 "The Blind Man Catches a Bird" in *The Girl Who Married a Lion: And Other Tales of Africa* by Alexander McCall Smith (New York: Pantheon Books, 2004), p. 78-81.

Page 75 "The Lady's Loaf-Field" in *Gaelic Ghosts* by Sorche Nic Leodhas, (New York: Holt, Rinehart and Winston, 1963), p. 68-74.

Page 79 "The Clever Sheik of the Butana" in *The Clever Sheikh of the Butana and Other Stories: Sudanese Folktales,* retold by Ali Lutfi Abdallah (New York: Interlink Books, 1999), p. 21-22.

Page 81 "Strawberries" is retold by storyteller Gayle Ross from a traditional Cherokee legend. A published version can be found in James Mooney, *Myths of the Cherokee,* Annual report of the Bureau of American Ethnology to the Secretary of the Smithsonian Institution; 19th, pt. 1; 1897-98. Other sources: *The First Strawberries: A Cherokee Story,* retold by Joseph Bruchac. (New York: Dial Books for Young Readers, 1993).

Page 86 "Why Wisdom is Found Everywhere" in *The Hat-Shaking Dance and Other Ashanti Tales from Ghana* by Harold Courlander with Albert Kofi Prempeh. (New York, Harcourt Brace, 1957.) Introductory notes are from Wikipedia: http://en.wikipedia.org/wiki/Anansi.

Page 88 "The Wise Quail" in *The Hungry Tigress: Buddhist Legends, Myths and Jataka Tales.* Told and with commentaries by Rafe Martin. (Cambridge, Massachusetts: Yellow Moon Press, 1999). Storyteller Rafe Martin graciously gave his permission to use this story, one I have told many times.

Page 92 "The Burning of the Rice Fields" is retold by Margo McLoughlin from Lafcadio Hearn, *Gleanings From the Buddha-Field.* (London: Kegan, Paul, Trench, Trubner & Company Limited, 1897). I first heard a version of this story from Victoria storyteller Jennifer Ferris. She told it shortly after the *tsunami* struck Japan in the spring of 2011. The piece in the story that most impressed me was the moment when Hamaguchei Gohei recalls the story he heard as a child and realizes the significance of the sea being pulled away from the land.

Page 97 "All Things Are Connected" in *Eleven Nature Tales: A Multicultural Journey* by Pleasant DeSpain. (Little Rock, Arkansas, 1996), p. 13-16. Introductory notes were inspired by "Through Ambiguous Tales: Women's Voices in Chokwe Storytelling" by Rachel I. Fretz in *Oral Tradition* 9/1 (1994): 230-250.

Acknowledgements

Grateful acknowledgment is made to the following publishers and storytellers for permission to print original material or to reprint and adapt from previously published material.

August House Publishers: "The Friendship Orchard" and "All Things Are Connected" from *Eleven Nature Tales, A Multicultural Journey* by Pleasant DeSpain. Copyright © 1999 Pleasant DeSpain. Published by August House Publishers, Inc. and used by permission of Marian Reiner on their behalf.

Bess Press: "How the Kangaroo Got Her Pouch" from *Pacific Island Legends: Tales from Micronesia, Melanesia, Polynesia, and Australia* by Bo Flood, Beret E. Strong, and William Flood. Reprinted by permission.

Hollym Corporation: "An Ox for a Persimmon" and "The Value of Salt" from *Korean Folk and Fairy Tales* retold by Suzanne Crowder Han. Text copyright © 1991, 2006 by Suzanne Crowder Han. Text printed by permission of Hollym Corporation; Publishers, Seoul, Korea.

Rafe Martin: "The Wise Quail" from *The Hungry Tigress: Buddhist Legends and Jataka Tales*, retold by Rafe Martin. Reprinted by permission of the author.

Random House: "A Drum," copyright © 1991 by A.K. Ramanujan, from *Folktales from India* by A.K. Ramanujan, copyright © 1991 by A.K. Ramanujan and "A Blind Man Catches a Bird": from *The Girl Who Married a Lion: and Other Tales from Africa* by Alexander McCall Smith, copyright © 1989, 1999, 2004 by Alexander McCall Smith. Used by permission of Pantheon Books, a division of Random House, Inc. Any third party use of this material, outside of this publication, is prohibited. Interested parties must apply directly to Random House, Inc. for permission.

Gayle Ross: "The Bird That Was Ashamed of Its Feet" and "Strawberries" are both traditional Cherokee stories, retold by storyteller Gayle Ross and reprinted with her permission.

Phyllis Soles: "The Christmas Doll" is published in this collection for the first time. Grateful acknowledgment is made to Phyllis Soles of Texada Island, British Columbia.

Sterling Publishers: "Buffalo Into Rooster" from *Folktales of Maharashtra* by Indumati Sheorey. Reprinted by permission.

The stories in this anthology come from many sources, including the living oral tradition of indigenous peoples. I gratefully acknowledge Cherokee storyteller Gayle Ross for allowing me to reprint two stories from the Cherokee tradition: "The Bird That Was Ashamed of Its Feet" and "Strawberries." Cultural appropriation continues to be an issue of great concern to all indigenous peoples. Likewise, there is a great need for truth telling in the portrayal of the First Nations of this continent, their experience during the period of European settlement, and their current experience as citizens of Canada, the United States, and Mexico. It is my hope, as editor of this anthology, that teachers and educators will use some or all of the stories as a springboard for discussion of cultural uniqueness and cultural similarities. Teachers can find additional information and resources at the following sites: http://americanindiansinchildrensliterature.blogspot.com/ and http://oyate.org/.

This manuscript was completed while I was Artist-in-Residence at the Centre for Studies in Religion and Society at the University of Victoria during the 2011 – 2012 academic year. I extend my heartfelt gratitude to the director, Paul Bramadat and to the staff— Leslie Kenny, Rina Langford-Kimmett and June Thomson. I would also like to thank Professor Yvonne Hsieh for her generous gift to the Centre, which allowed the creation of the Chih-Chuang and Yien-Ying Hsieh Award for Art and Spirituality. Thank you to my readers Abegael Fisher-Lang and Stephen Kagan for their valuable suggestions, to Leslie Kenny for her editing skill and to Carol Neufeld for proof-reading. Four teachers at Willows Elementary School in Victoria welcomed me into their classrooms to try out my storytelling series. Thank you to Sondra Showers, Tanya Foster, Alissa O'Rourke and Marilyn Fox. Thanks as well to their students for being such good listeners.

This project was funded by the John E. Fetzer Institute in Kalamazoo, Michigan. The Fetzer Institute also funded the companion CD *The Giving Heart: Tales of Generosity from Near and Far* as well as a guide for using stories in community, *The Giving Heart: Folktales for Exploring Generosity.* Many thanks to Mark Nepo for dreaming the Generosity of Spirit project into being, and to Ian Simmons for bringing me on board. A number of colleagues at the Fetzer Institute have contributed to the material in this collection, including Ian Simmons, Wayne Muller, Megan Scribner, and Pat Harbour. A deep bow of gratitude to you all. Many thanks also to Deborah Higgins and Jackie Stack for your support of this project. Many storytellers have shaped my thinking about storytelling and its role in education. Thank you to Johanna Kuyvenhoven, Pat Carfra, Jennifer Ferris, Abegael Fisher-Lang, Diane Gilliland, Anne Glover, Peg Hasted, Shoshana Litman, Faye Mogensen, Melanie Ray, Dan Yashinsky, Doug Lipman, and Jay O'Callahan.

Resources

Storytelling and Education

Eder, Donna with Regina Holyan. 2010. *Life Lessons Through Storytelling: Children's Exploration of Ethics.* Bloomington, IN: Indiana University Press.

Fox Eades, Jennifer M. 2006. *Classroom Tales: Using Storytelling to Build Emotional, Social and Academic Skills Across the Primary Curriculum.* London: Jessica Kingsley Publishers.

Hamilton, Martha and Mitch Weiss, Beauty & the Beast Storytellers. *Children Tell Stories: A Teaching Guide.* Katonah, New York: Richard C. Owen Publishers, Inc. 1990, following Beauty & the Beast Storytellers.

Kinghorn, Harriet R. and Mary Helen Pelton. 1991. *Every Child a Storyteller: A Handbook of Ideas.* Englewood, Colorado: Teachers Ideas Press.

Kuyvenhoven, Johanna. 2009. *In the Presence of Each Other: A Pedagogy of Storytelling.* Toronto, ON: University of Toronto Press.

McEwan, Hunter and Kieran Egan. Eds. 1995. *Narrative in Teaching, Learning, and Research.* New York, NY: Teachers College Press.

Storytelling and Story Collections

Lipman, Doug. 1999. *Improving Your Storytelling: Beyond the Basics for All Who Tell Stories in Work or Play.* Little Rock, Arkansas: August House Press.

Read MacDonald, Margaret. 1992. *Peace Tales: World Folktales to Talk About.* Little Rock, Arkansas: August House Publishers.

_____. 1999. *Earth Care: World Folktales to Talk About.* North Haven, CT: Linnet Books.

Miller, Teresa with assistance from Anne Pellowski. Edited by Norma Livo. Introduction by Laura Simms. 1988. *Joining In: An Anthology of Audience Participation Stories & How to Tell Them.* Cambridge, MA: Yellow Moon Press.

Seeds of Generosity Newsletter

Sign up for the newsletter to share your own ideas and to receive blog-posts about the application of storytelling in the classroom. Visit www.margostoryteller.net.